Myth Coloring Book

Myth Coloring Book

DENNIS RALPH ARCHAMBAULT, PHD

Mythology, With A Depth Psychology Emphasis

Cover By Ila Rose | *Illustrations By* Jesse Springer

Printed in the United States of America

Cover Design by Melissa Lund, Luminare Press
Cover Artwork by Ila Rose
Illustrations by Jesse Springer

Dance-N-Life Publishing, LLC
1555 Coburg Road
Suite 77
Eugene, Oregon 97401
MythColoringBook.com

LCCN: TXu 2-088-549
ISBN: 978-0-9729752-2-3

Additional Copies and Illustrations
MythColoringBook.com

In the Beginning...

MythColoringBook has been created for your delight and self-discovery.

Mythology and ritual has been a part of our human heritage from 200,000 to 75,000 BC. Discoveries in Switzerland and the German Alps of cave-bear skulls, altars, workable flints, and, the remnants of charcoal show the first evidence of the use of fire.*

MythColoringBook offers 21 common images and symbols to color preceded by world wide mythological interpretations for each image. You are invited to discover your own mythology in: the "why" of a Flood, Moon or Mountain Myth, or the "meaning" of the Water, Rock, Fire or Tree Myth, or the "wherefore" of the Cloud, Cosmic Egg or another mythic image.

When you take the time to *expressively* color each mythic image, your conscious mind will be so engaged that your deep inner wisdom is freed to "bubble up" as you reflect on what you have read. Being otherwise busy is how great ideas suddenly pop into our mind whether in the shower, awakening from a dream, doing gardening or engaging other activities.

Reflecting on your life, as it has been, is now, and what you would like it to be, is the self-discovery opportunity available to you as you color the images and symbols in *MythColoringBook*.

What myths are you living? How are your myths different from other storytellers who have gone before you? Importantly, your meanings serve your life more than theirs. So...what are your stories?

That adventure awaits you within these pages. Have fun and...

Color yourself mythic!

*Joseph Campbell, *The Mythic Dimension: Selected Essays* 1957-1987

About the Illustrations

The illustrations in *MythColoringBook* are minimalistic. They offer simple elements with little embellishments. By this approach, the mythic images to be colored are different from those available in other coloring books that require exactitude to the areas to be filled-in. Such constraints are avoided in order to allow your unencumbered artistry to flourish. Auras are welcomed!

Be free! The sky can be green while grass can be blue, or purple or any number of choices. It all depends upon what you sense while reading the mythic background for each image. In other words, avoid being rigidly color correct; be courageous and reject "the way things are" if that is what your creativity needs in order to thrive.

MythColoringBook encourages you to be large and unhindered. Welcome all impulses that arise. This is how your mythic uniqueness will be discovered.

It is unlikely that you will discover your own mythology by being defined by someone else or by being inhibited by "must be like." And, some people are inspired by words rather than images; if a mythic subject stimulates a series of words or phrases to be written around the image, so be it. Honor that which arises in you.

MythColoringBook is about you. Be BOLD and MYTHIC!

Acknowledgements

I want to acknowledge Nancy Bright, (https://brightcreationsart.com/), for the early rendition of my concept of the Cosmic Egg and Ila Rose's, (https://ilaroseart.bigcartel.com/), exceptional enrichment of that vision as it is displayed on the front cover.

Margaret Merisante, PhD, https://www.mythwoman.com, a feminist comparative mythologist colleague and good friend, was a delight to work with as she proofread *MythColoringBook*. Look for her upcoming book on Goddesses.

My appreciation is extended to Nyhetsbyran, Stockholm SE, (https://tt.se/en/lennart-nilsson/), for the license of the womb photo in the Tree Myth. It is my belief that we love trees, and especially laying under canopies looking up through them, because they remind us of the time we were in the womb. Turn to the Tree Myth and see for yourself. Notice how the mother's veins and tree branches mirror one another!

Luminare Press, (https://www.luminarepress.com/), was a joy to work with, especially Melissa Lund and her brilliant graphic concepts. They create book designs needed for hard copy and electronic printing. I highly recommend them to all first time, or repeat, authors for their publishing needs.

Lastly, I extend my gratitude to the Pacifica Graduate Institute, (https://www.pacifica.edu/), in Carpinteria, California whose Mythology program, with a Depth Psychology Emphasis, bestowed upon us the wisdom of our species as found in mythology and depth psychology. It is the only doctoral program in the country dedicated to the exploration of human experience through the interdisciplinary and multicultural study of myth, ritual, religion, literature, depth psychology and art.

Table of Contents

The Bridge Myth

The Bridge Myth is a symbol of crossing or linking two opposite sides, physical or imaginal.

Bridges offer passage over raging waters, safety across perilous landscapes and over busy streets using a skyway bridge. They aid travelers by their convenience. Bridges also have metaphoric meanings when they join, connect or transition: as in closing the gap between two sets of beliefs, two people, changing conditions or other sets of opposites.

Rainbows are a universal mythologized symbol of celestial bridges from Earth to Heaven, and reverse. In a spiritual tradition, they connect the individual with the divine. Explaining this, Arnold Van Gennep writes in *The Rites of Passage* that, "A rite of spatial (physical space) passage has become a rite of spiritual passage." Often actual sacrifices, human at first, then animal, were performed at bridge dedications. Destructive spirits and energies were placated so that these structures would remain intact and their travelers not be cast down to their deaths. Mircea Eliade writes in *The Myth of the Eternal Return* that, "construction rituals repeat the primordial act of the cosmogonic [universe's] construction." Religious traditions imagine the bridge as being as narrow as a sword's, razor's or knife's edge or being as thin as a thread upon which the traveler must walk. Those who lived lives of merit would make the crossing successfully, while those whose lives were not well lived were cast down to their deaths and into hell.

Bridges also have a psychological interpretation of connecting the conscious with the unconscious, the ego with the psyche. Dreams bridge the dreamworld with the daytime world as they reflect the inner experience as it relates to the outer reality. Shamans must go where "night and day meet." Mircea Eliade writes in *Shamanism: Archaic Techniques of Ecstasy* that shamans, "like the dead, must cross a bridge in the course of their journey to the underworld." In the initiatory symbolism of the "strait gate" or of a "paradoxical passage," Eliade states that shamans must "transcend opposites [and] abolish the polarity typical of the human condition in order to attain the ultimate reality." In *Two Essays on Analytical Psychology*, Carl Jung writes "from a consideration of the claims of the inner and outer worlds, or rather, from the conflict between them, the possible and the necessary follows. Unfortunately, our Western mind, lacking all cultures in this respect, has never yet devised a concept, nor even a name, for the union of opposites through the middle path, that most fundamental item of inward experience, which could respectably be set against the Chinese concept of Tao. It is at once the most individual fact and the most universal, the most legitimate fulfillment of the meaning of the individual's life."

Another title for the Catholic Pope is Roman Pontiff, coming from the ancient Roman College of Pontiffs, *Pontifex Maximus*, which means greatest bridge builder. In Japanese mythology, brother and sister creation deities, Izanagi no-Mikoto and Izanami no-Mikoto were told to create land and life. Standing on the "floating bridge of heaven" they stirred the waters of the sea with a lance which the gods had given them and the islands of Japan came into being.

QUESTIONS FOR REFLECTION AS YOU COLOR THE BRIDGE

1. How does the Bridge Myth relate to your life?

2. What is being sought in the opposite that you seek?

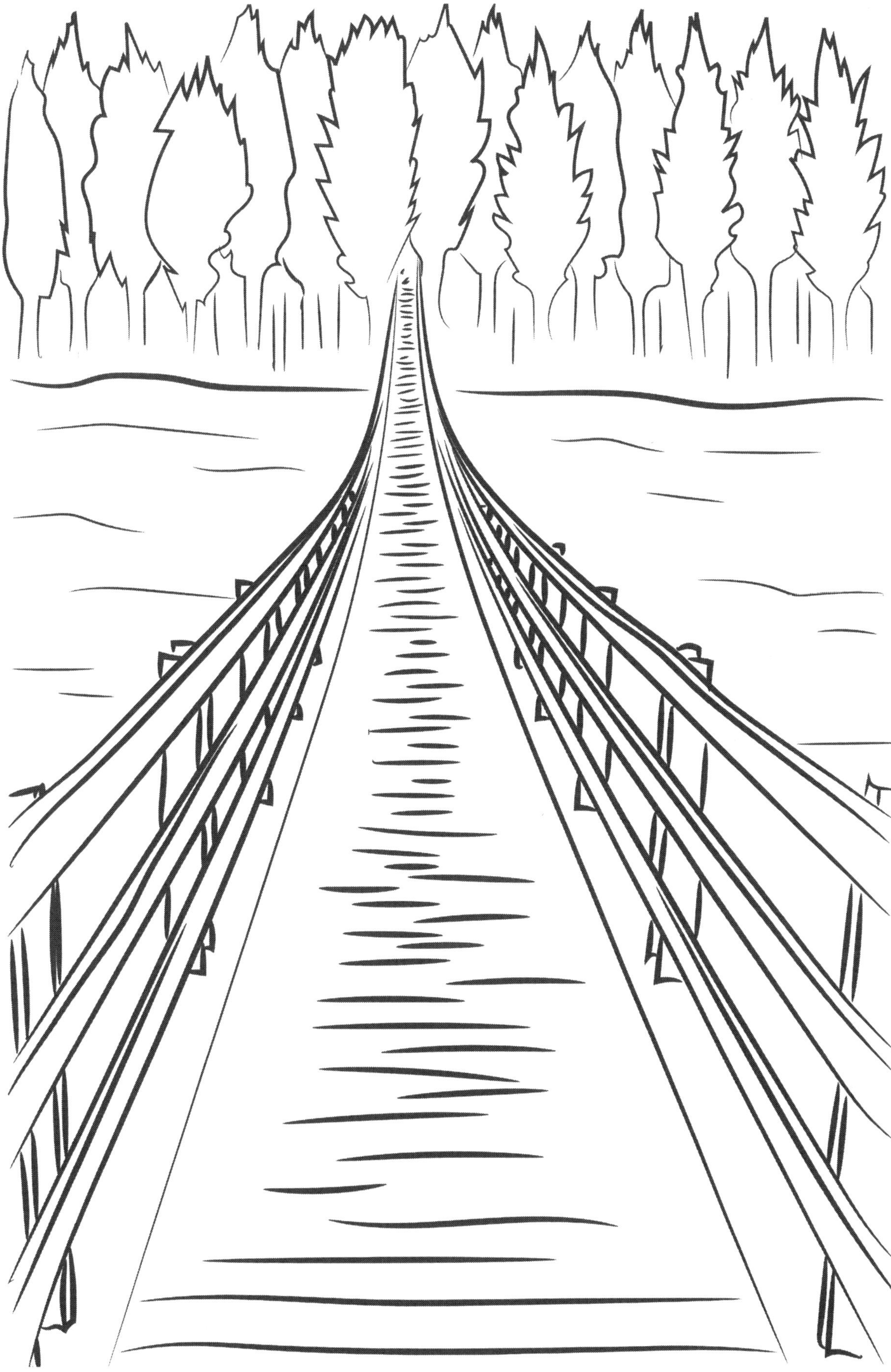

The Butterfly Myth

The Butterfly is a mythic image of transformation and re-birth, especially from the chrysalis (cocoon) stage into the majestic butterfly.

Psychologically, the butterfly symbolizes an individual's freedom from old life patterns and attitudes from manipulative personalities and beliefs. As such, the butterfly is the symbol of the soul in Europe, central Asia, New Zealand, Zaire and Mexico. Mythic stories from Mycenae in 1500 BC represent the butterfly as the Great Mother Goddess. For the Chinese, butterflies were symbols of immortality; for the ancient Greeks they were the symbol of the psyche in the myth of Eros and Psyche. Depicted in jade jewelry in Japan, butterflies represent the wedding of souls. They were also symbols of resurrection for the early Christians and are found on their ancient tombs.

The Monarch butterfly is named after Danaus, the mythical king of Egypt and son of Zeus. Their transformation lasts about 6–8 weeks: from an egg, to a caterpillar, to a chrysalis and finally to the butterfly. They live for about 9 months. As a caterpillar, they must eat enough plant life to last their entire lifetime because as a butterfly they will drink only nectar, which has no protein or fat.

The scales on the butterfly give it its colors. Pigments of melanin give the black and browns, uric acid derivatives and flavones give them yellows, and their own micro-structures of scales and hairs provide the iridescent blues, greens and reds. Butterflies see polarized light which allows them to navigate in cloudy conditions. It is estimated that butterflies evolved from moths 30-60 million years ago. There are approximately 18,000 species of butterflies. Moths are mostly nocturnal (night), whereas butterflies are diurnal (day) insects. They migrate over thousands of miles.

In contemporary depth psychology, the emerging butterfly is seen as the act of individuation which separates itself from collective social structure in order to grow into consciousness of Self. In dreams, one interpretation is that butterflies are encounters with liberation and new life. In *Symbols of Transformation*, Carl Jung writes that "...the butterfly is a symbol and allegory [story] of the psyche." In *Psychological Types,* Jung defines the psyche "as being the totality of all psychic processes, conscious as well as unconscious." This loosely embraces all feelings, the will, and that which is spiritual and instinctual. In *Anatomy of the Psyche*, Edward F. Edinger suggests that the individual psyche must be whole in order to stand against the outer world in order to fulfill its task of being a carrier of consciousness.

QUESTIONS FOR REFLECTION AS YOU COLOR THE BUTTERFLY

1. How does the Butterfly Myth relate to your life?

2. Where does your mystical flight of renewal alight?

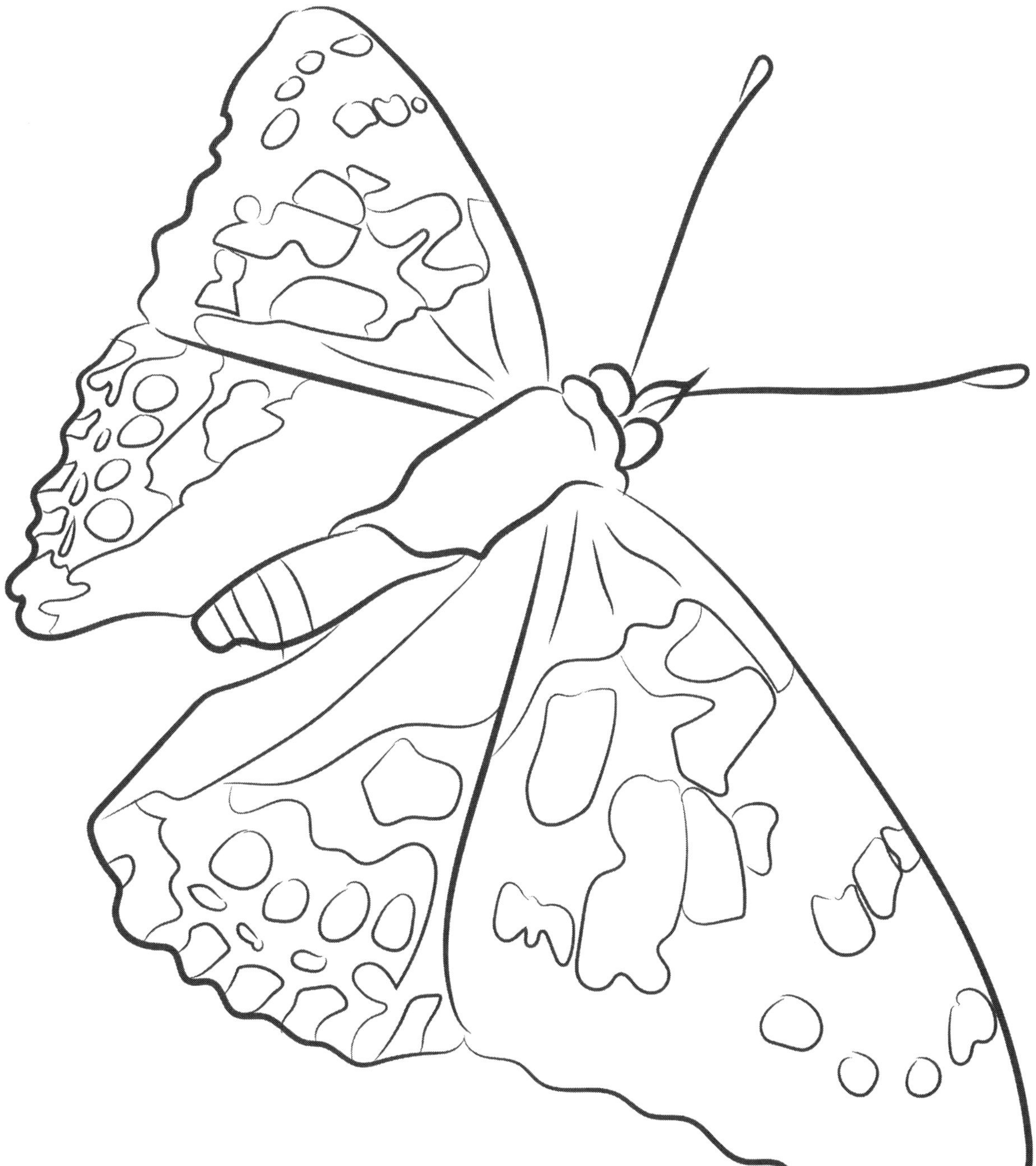

The Cloud Myth

The Cloud myth is one of divinity, fertility, comfort…and they can be delightfully fun to watch.

Clouds inspire all ages to "see" faces, animals, angels, symbols and other imaginal creatures. All that is needed are two dark spots for eyes, one for the nose and another for the mouth. With that, the theater of the mind has been cast.

In a 16th century treatise, Theobald de Hoghelande writes, "…we sometimes imagine in the clouds or in the fire strange shapes of animals, reptiles, or trees." Your own deep psychological state may be revealed by whether they are friendly or threatening. An unhappy person in a dark mood is distressed, deeply anxious or "under a cloud of suspicion."

Clouds give us relief on hot summer days and offer the promise of rain for all. Clouds naturally occur from the earth's hot surface where water vapor gathers on dust particles. They rise and condense high in the atmosphere. In their fullness, they bring the promise of rain, but in their lurking densities in the upper regions, they threaten us with hail and terrible storms.

Their complex formations beckon us to "project" into them. Projection, defined by Marie-Louise von Franz in *Projection and Re-collection in Jungian Psychology*, is "that which is an unperceived and unintentional transfer of subjective psychic elements into an outer object." It is the way that we envision imaginal images when none really exist. Aristotle thought clouds are one form of the *prima materia* or first matter. Carl Jung writes in *Aion*, that *prima materia* is an "intuitive concept for an *initial psychic situation*, symbolized by such terms as water of life, cloud, heaven, shadow, dragon…" He also writes in *Psychology and Alchemy* that "*Prima materia* can be found always and everywhere." This is the foundation for all the stories we tell about ourselves and others, in our projections, which may persist throughout all of our lives with benevolence or with injustice.

World mythologies and religions have rich traditions with clouds, abounding as they do in mountain tops, such as on Olympus and Mt Sinai. Clouds can represent divinity, god, god's energy, god's messengers, and heavenly blessings or punishments. *Genesis 9:13* states: "I do set my [rain]bow in the cloud, and it shall be a token of a covenant between me and the earth." Rabanus Maurus, a Frankish Benedictine monk (780-856 AD), writes that "the cloud represents the comfort of the Holy Ghost and Christ's ascension." Additionally, *Qur'ān 24:43* states that, "Seest thou that Allah makes the clouds move gently, then joins them together, then makes them into a heap, then wilt thou see rain issue forth."

Artists are inspired by clouds. In a 10th century painting [artist unknown], the angel Gabriel, dressed in blue and white robes, is surrounded by swirling pink clouds. He is revealing to the Virgin Mary that it is God's will that she conceive his only child, Jesus Christ. In another 10th century painting of a Chinese divinity, Avalokitesvara (Sanskrit meaning the "Lord who contemplates" and "embodying the compassion of all Buddhas") sweeps down from a purple cloud to guide the soul of a newly deceased devotee.

QUESTIONS FOR REFLECTION AS YOU COLOR THE CLOUD

1. How does the Cloud Myth relate to your life?

2. When did you last see faces and images in clouds?

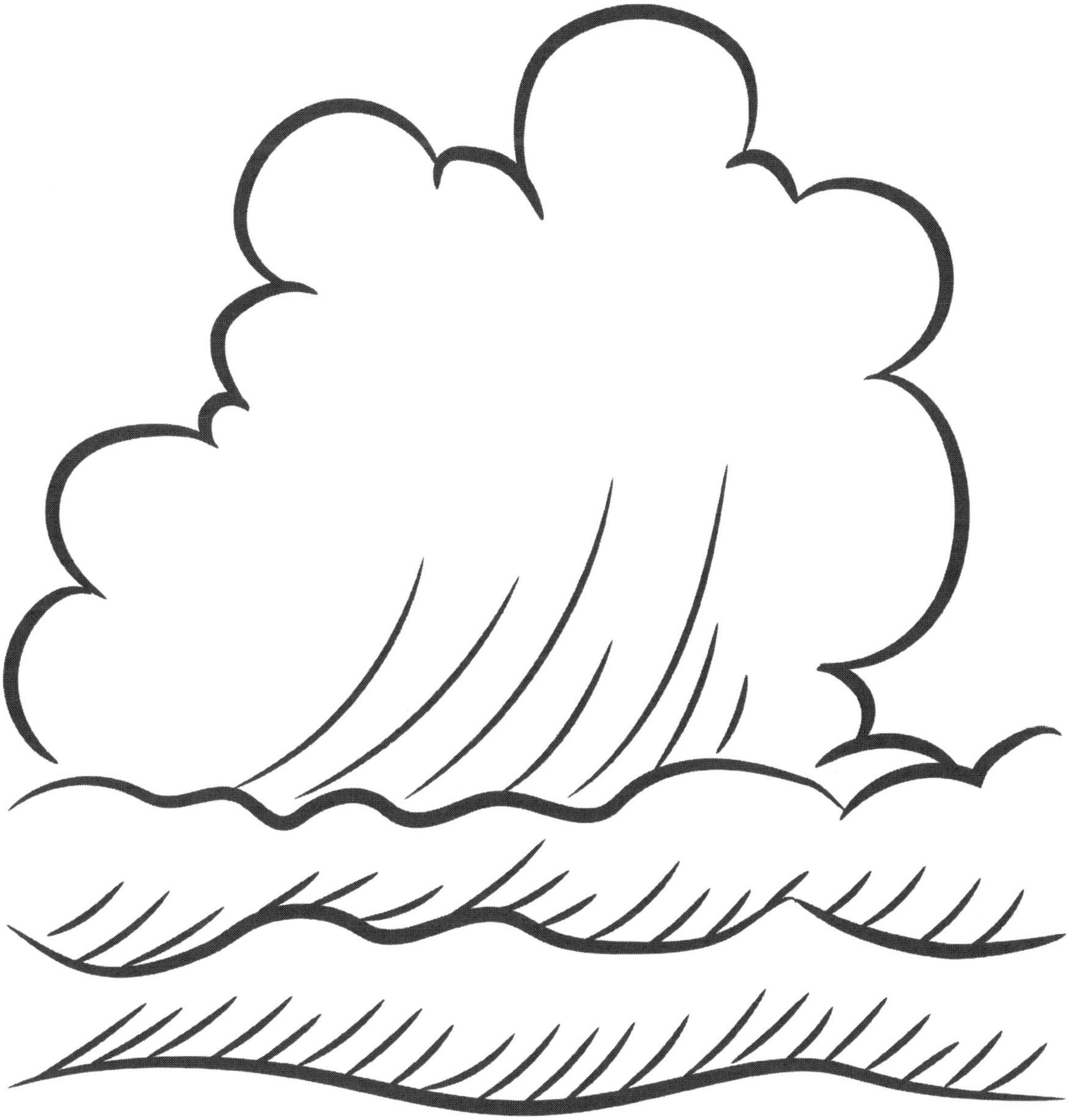

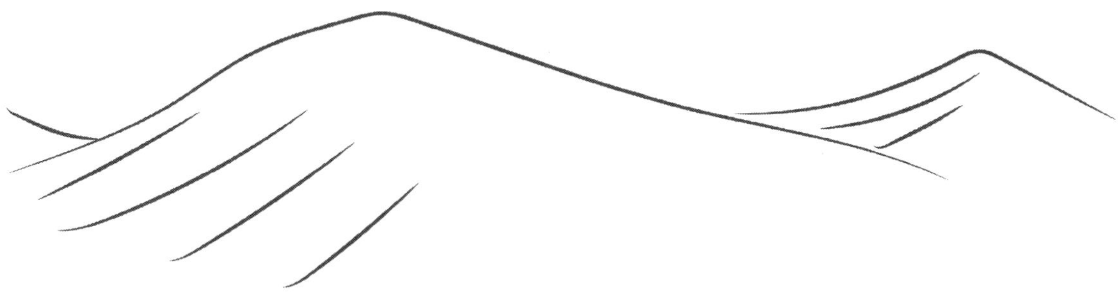

The Cosmic Egg Myth

The Cosmic Egg symbolizes a new beginning, the world's creation or a rebirth of a divine origin.

Mircea Eliade writes in *Patterns in Comparative Religion* that the Cosmic Egg is "a rebirth modelled on the creation of the world." In Eastern spiritual traditions, the soul is believed to be inside the egg, floating in the ocean of life (*Prana*) emerging from nature (*Prakriti*), and taking the name Brahma. It becomes the original maker of materiality. Eric Neumann writes in *The Great Mother*, "thus in many world mythologies we encounter the egg as the archetypal [model] symbol of world creation." Carl Jung adds in *Symbols of Transformation* that, "the world is enclosed in the egg… [and] is the cosmic birth-giver…"

In the Middle Ages, alchemical texts consider the egg to be the natural philosopher's vessel from which the spiritual, inner and complete human is found. The Cosmic Egg (to be colored) represents the still moment of the egg prior to birth, as Joseph Campbell writes in *The Hero with a Thousand Faces*, "an awesome figure in human form that is to be."

The Chimú of ancient Peru believe that heroes and humankind originate in the egg. In India, Prajāpati is the self-begotten egg–the cosmic egg from which he hatches himself. This Hindu deity creeps into himself, becomes his own womb and makes himself pregnant with himself in order to hatch forth the world of multiplicity. The Polynesian islanders of Anaa believe that the universe was originally an egg containing Te Tumu (the prototypical male) and Te Papa (the prototypical female). In a Hawaiian origin myth, a bird laid an egg upon the primeval waters and afterward burst itself out to produce the world.

Throughout world mythologies, the cosmic egg is the embodiment of life essence as well as a relief from the bewilderment of corporal [physical body] existence seeking spiritual manifestation. It is perhaps a description of the state of chaos which the Greeks named "cosmos." According to Oswald Spengler, who writes in *The Decline of the West*, this understanding of cosmos became, in the classical age, the "harmonic order which includes each separate thing as a well-defined, comprehensible and present entity."

Egyptologist E. A. Wallis Budge notes in his translation of the *Papyrus of ANI*, in his *Book of the Dead*, that, "[Osiris] rises up out of the Egg in the Hidden Land." Osiris, the dying and resurrected god in Egyptian mythology, is thus also held in the cosmic egg.

A southeastern Borneo myth tells

of the world being made by spreading earth on the head of the great serpent Ndengei who swims in a primeval sea. Another deity descends and discovers seven eggs. Taking two of these eggs, breaking them open, he finds in one a fully formed man and in the other a fully formed woman. However, both are lifeless. Ndengei returns to the upper world and asks the creator for breath that both might come alive. The creator grants this breath and both are brought to life.

QUESTIONS FOR REFLECTION AS YOU COLOR THE COSMIC EGG

1. How does the Cosmic Egg Myth relate to your life?

2. What Beloved within you seeks to be born?

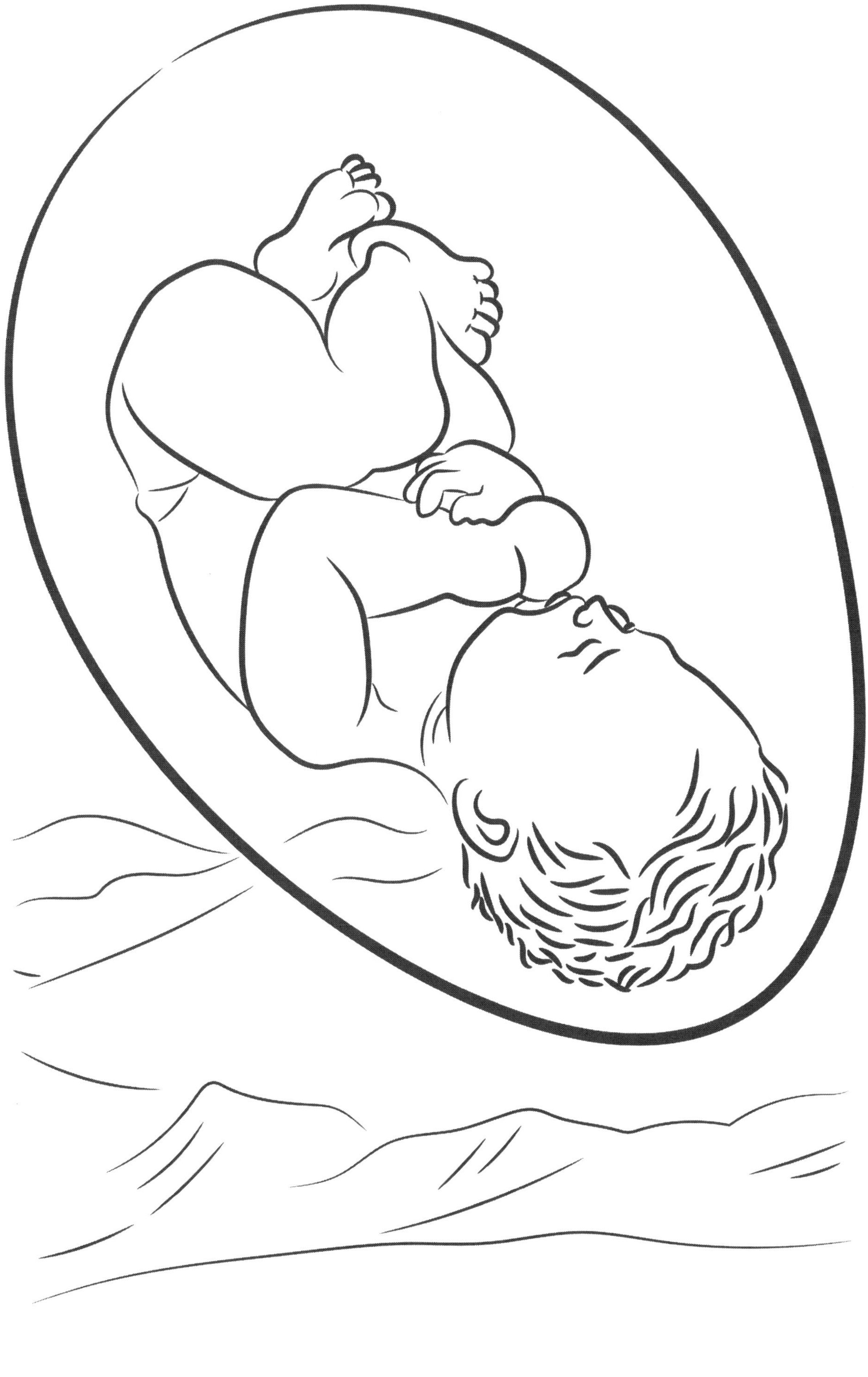

The Crossroads Myth

Crossroads are symbols of transition, hazards, holy places, new directions and fate's destiny from forced decisions.

Significant psychological changes are implied at intersections. The junction of two or more roads at a single point holds mystical and religious meanings throughout world mythology. The intersection of three roads were especially dangerous, yet sacred. This tri-fold junction was believed by ancient Greeks to hold profound mystical power–being under the dominion of the underworld goddess Hecate and the god Hermes. Both are psychopomps–guides to the spirits of the dead to the underworld. Karl Kerenyi writes in *Hermes: Guide of Souls* that Hermes "is constantly underway: he is *enodios* (by the road) and *hodios* (belonging to a journey) and one encounters him on every path." Arnold Van Gennep writes in *The Rites of Passage* that "...to cross the threshold is to unite oneself with a new world."

Sophocles' play *Oedipus the King* follows the story of Oedipus who unknowingly fulfills his fate by killing his father. On his journey to avoid this prophecy, he is assaulted by a stranger on the road. Oedipus kills him and later discovers that the man, indeed, was his father, Laius. Sophocles notes that this assault was "at a place where three highways meet."

The ancient Greeks made sacrifices at these junctions, as well as disposing there the corpses of suicides and criminals executed for felonies. In this way, they believed that the spirits of these individuals could not find their way back home.

Also, *Ezekiel 21:21* states: "For the king of Babylon stands at the parting of the way, at the fork in the two roads, to use divination; he shakes the arrows, he consults the teraphim [a religious image expected to convey messages to the living] and inspects the [animal] liver."

Ancient Rome paid homage to crossroad spirits by erecting a combination of obelisks, altars, stones, chapels and inscriptions at crossroads. Herm stone statues, the origin of the name *Hermes*, were boundary markers placed at these intersections. These statues depicted a bearded man without arms, but with an erect phallus. This symbolized life-giving energy which protected travelers. The Roman god Janus, the two-faced god who looks in opposite directions, is also placed at intersections to warn travelers of unseen dangers. In *The Lives of Noble Grecians and Romans*, Plutarch, writing about Rome's legendary king Numa Pompilius, says, "For this Janus, whether in remote antiquity he was a demigod or a king, was certainly a great lover of civil and social unity, and one who reclaimed men from brutal and savage living; for which reason they figure him with two faces, to represent the two states and conditions out of the one of which he brought mankind, to lead them into the other."

Carl Jung observes in his *Symbols of Transformation* that, "where the roads cross and enter into one another, thereby symbolizing the union of opposites, there is the "mother," the object and epitome of all union." We see this today with statues of the Madonna at crossroads, as well as those with crosses and saint's images.

QUESTIONS FOR REFLECTION AS YOU COLOR THE CROSSROADS

1. How does the Crossroads Myth relate to your life?

2. What direction does your Higher Self want you to go now?

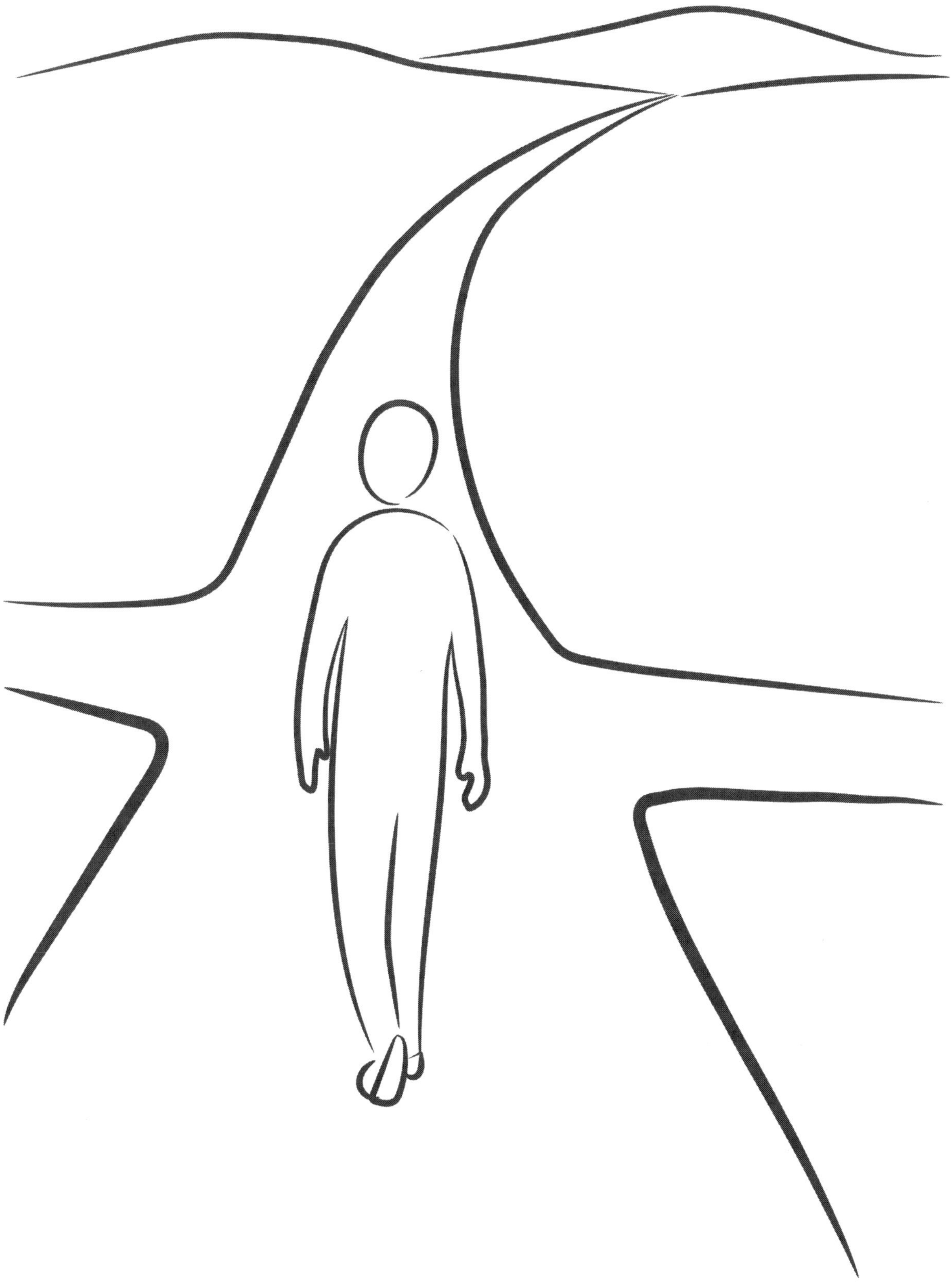

The Earthrise Myth

Earthrise photos show our beautiful, blue water planet in the black void of space that is home to humans and multitudes of life forms.

This is the new mythology for our time. No territorial boundaries exist and all cultures are united in the potential of life supported by this living planet. The stunning photographs, taken from the Moon, reveal our beautiful home with its green living matter, brown soil and blue water surrounded by moving white cloud formations set against the black immensity of lifeless near-space.

Gods and goddesses have been worshipped since the earliest times, and the first were those reflecting our reverence of the Earth. Marija Gimbutas writes in *The Language of the Goddess*, that "caves, crevices and caverns of the Earth are natural manifestations of the primordial womb of the Mother. This idea is not Neolithic in origin; it goes back to the Paleolithic, when the narrow passages, oval-shaped areas, clefts and small cavities of caves are marked or painted entirely in red." The Earth symbolizes motherhood. Sigmund Freud writes in *Group Psychology*, "the series of gods, then, would run chronologically: Mother Goddess—Hero—Father God." In *Moses and Monotheism*, Freud writes, "At a point in this evolution which is not easily determined, great mother-goddesses appeared, probably even before male gods, and afterwards persisted for a long time beside them."

There have been Earth goddesses in all cultures. The Sumerians had Ninhursag, the Akkadians, Ishtar or Innana, Hindus had Prithvi, Polynesians had Papa, Africans had Ala and Ibo, and the Greeks had Gaia. In *Theogony*, Hesiod writes, "Gaia even gave birth to Heaven (Ouranos) who then had to impregnate her to give birth to all the gods. First of all, Chaos came into being; but next was wide-breasted Gaia, always a safe foundation of all immortals who possess the peaks of snowy Olympos..."

Aeschylus wrote about Earth in the play, *Choephoroe*, "she that gave us birth." In *Job 1:21*, identifying Mother Earth with the womb, is written, "naked I came out of my mother's womb, and naked shall I return thither." The Earth is seen as maternal and protective and a symbol of fertility and sustenance, as well as our final resting place.

Written in *The Excerpta Ex Theodoto of Clement of Alexandria* is, "therefore man is in man not consisting as part to part but united as whole to whole by God's unspeakable power." In *Genesis 1:2*, "the earth was a formless void and darkness covered the face of the deep" and later in *Genesis 1:9*, "and God said, 'let the waters under the sky be gathered together into one place, and let the dry land appear. And it was so and God called the dry land Earth.'"

Many native American Indian mythologies have stories of earth-divers who created the land from the deep waters. The Athabaskan, Blackfoot, Chippewa, Cree, Mohawk, Nipmuc, Ojibway and Potawatomi all have a muskrat as an earth-diver. The Ottawa have both the muskrat and the coot performing this task. The Gros Ventre and the Arapaho have a turtle as the earth-diver while the Cayuga have a toad creating habitable land.

New discoveries are revealing how microbial substances from soil bacteria and fungi have healing qualities which we are just now beginning to cultivate. Earth is in our own time becoming not only the womb of our birth but our healer as well.

QUESTIONS FOR REFLECTION AS YOU COLOR THE EARTHRISE

1. How does the Earthrise Myth relate to your life?

2. Are you inspired to a global consciousness?

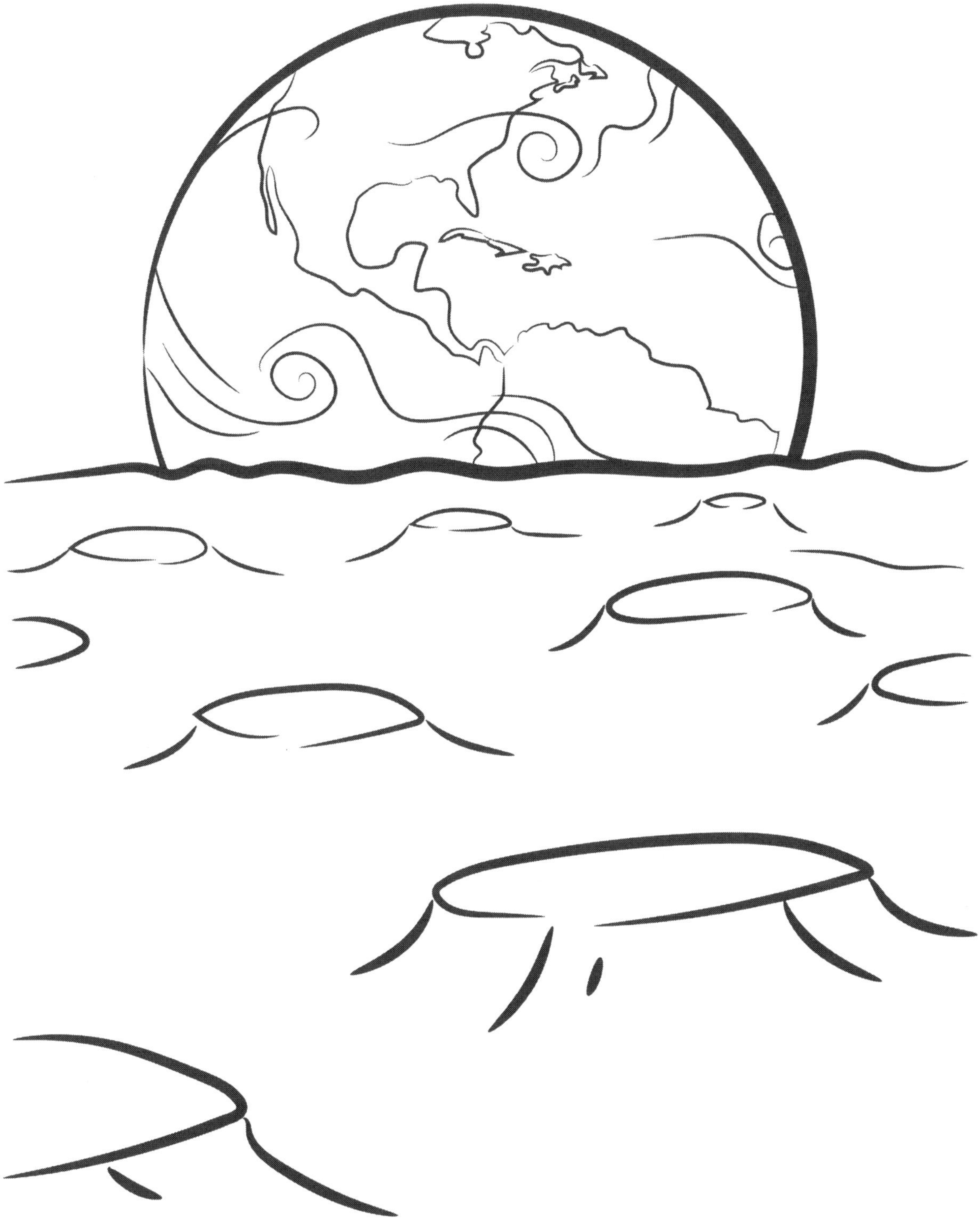

The Fire Myth

The Fire myth is a symbol of a destructive power harnessed for human betterment.

Fire has been the center of tribal and community gatherings since ancient times. The creation of fire by rubbing two sticks together marks one of the most impressive accomplishments of our species. Prior to this discovery, only lightning or volcanoes provided fire to humans. Fire gives us heat, light and energy. Life always grows abundantly from ashes. Additionally, fibrous meats and vegetables are rendered edible and a communal fire is the gathering place for developing lasting bonds of kinship and family.

Mythically, Friedrich Nietzsche writes in *The Birth of Tragedy* that humans not only receive fire as a gift from heaven, as lightning or warming solar heat, but that it is also a "crime and robbery of the divine nature."

Flame is an essential element of shamanic practices. The ancient Greeks felt that fire purified their relations with the underworld and the dead. Finno-Ugric people also used fire for purification by jumping over it. Modern practices of walking on red hot coals to test one's mental state seems to be drawn from this. North American Indians believed that fire gives happiness and good fortune. Carl Jung writes in *The Structure and Dynamics of the Psyche* that among indigenous peoples "the soul is a fire or flame." In the *Mahabharata*, king Yudhishthira was challenged by the invisible voice of his deceased father to answer the question, "Who is the guest that all life is host to?" The answer given is "fire." In a rare twist, the heaven-dweller myths of the Wachaga of Africa and the myths of Polynesia's underworld have mortals teaching fire-making skills to the gods.

Both the ancient Greek god Zeus and the Iranian god Trita have a thunderbolt as a weapon. Also in the Trita myth, fire from heaven to earth prepared the intoxicating draught of immortality. The ancient Greek goddess Demeter uses the purifying element of fire for making humans immortal. The Water-Spider of the Cherokee nation snatches fire from where Thunder had concealed it in a sacred sycamore. The First People of the American West coast obtained precious fire by stealing it from a jealous watchman who pursues the thief. Relays of animals, however, carry the fire off successfully. The Piegan Blackfeet myth is similar to the First people myths in that the beaver and woodpecker steal fire from the salmon. The loss of fire in primitive times was a great misfortune, especially to the hunter gatherers.

A Chippewa prophet said, "...you must remember that the life in your body and the fire in your lodge are the same...if you suffer your fire to be extinguished, at that moment your life will be at its end."

The quintessential fire-rebirth symbol is the Phoenix which is born anew from its own ashes. Mircea Eliade writes in *Myths, Dreams, and Mysteries* that, "heat and fire, on the plane of mystical physiology, indicate the awakening of a magico-religious power." Marie-Louise von Franz writes in *On Dreams and Death* that, "an immortal one is born out of the womb of fire."

QUESTIONS FOR REFLECTION AS YOU COLOR THE FIRE

1. How does the Fire Myth relate to your life?

2. What burning passion in you wants to be liberated?

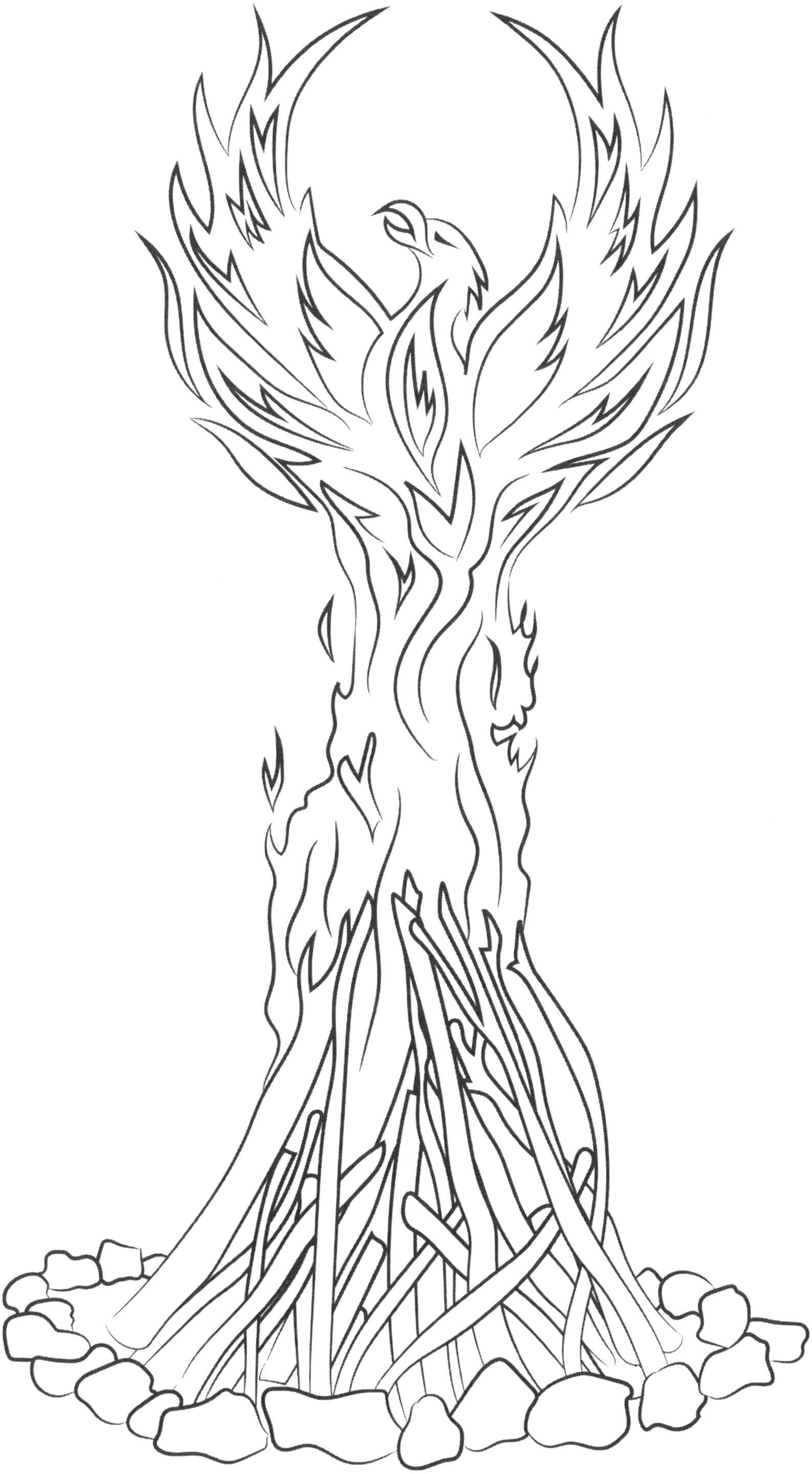

The Flood Myth

The Flood symbol is one of an unstoppable force.

Floods wash away landscapes and cause massive destruction. They have many natural sources: torrential rains, tsunamis, hurricanes and typhoons, as well as failures of sea barriers and dams. In certain cases, annual floods benefit new life by depositing rich soil that make the land more fertile, such as with the Nile floods.

In terms of human psychology, a person may be swamped by a "flood of emotions." In *Mythology of the Soul*, analytical psychologist H. G. Baynes writes of a patient that, "he looks down upon his flooded world. Were he to listen he might hear the cries of the solitary, marooned survivor, who is of course himself, the self that is threatened by the rising waters of the unconscious." Additionally, Edward F. Edinger writes in *Anatomy of the Psyche* that, "flood myths tell us explicitly, the flood comes from God; that is a "*solutio*" [loosening, dissolving] that comes from the Self. What is not worth saving is dissolved and melted down in order to be recast in new life-forms. Thus, the ongoing life process renews itself."

Africa, like the rest of the world, has flood and deluge mythologies. Some flood myths tell "nature myth" tales that provided early humans with an explanation for the massive waters. Other flood myths relate them to divine punishments for misbehaving, disobedient and violent humans.

The Congo people of Angola tell the myth of the sun who threw mud at the moon making it less bright, thus provoking an angry reaction and receiving a great flood in retaliation. The Akkadian *Epic of Gilgamesh*, compiled around 1200 BC which incorporates the Akkadian flood myths of Atra-Hasis tells the tale of three gods: Anu the sky god, Enlil the earth god and Enki the fresh water god. Due to human overpopulation and disturbance, Enlil decides to reduce the human population with a great flood. However, Enki warns the hero, Atra-Hasis by speaking through a reed wall, i.e., a heavenly voice oracle, to build a boat to escape and he is saved. Historically, the Atra-Hasis flood myth precedes the Biblical flood myth with Noah and his ark by several centuries.

In ancient southern Chinese mythology, a man catches the Thunder God who is responsible for global inundation. However, the man's children free the Thunder God and the floods return. The man floats upward to persuade the Lord of Heaven to stop the flooding and finally it is done. The Southeast Asian Chewong people suffer flooding because someone committed the cardinal sin of laughing at animals. This taboo vexes the Original Snake whose angry movements cause primeval waters to rise and drown everyone. Finally, in Norse mythology, the final battle of Ragnarok—the cataclysmic cosmic conflict that marks a new world beginning—begins when the world serpent, the Midgard Serpent, releases its tail. Midgard had been cast into the sea but had survived and grown so large that it encircles the earth. Swallowing its tail, Midgard becomes the first ouroboros, a symbol of wholeness or infinity. When the serpent releases its tail, widespread flooding drowns all inhabitants and poisonous gases are released. The waters recede eventually and life is renewed.

QUESTIONS FOR REFLECTION AS YOU COLOR THE FLOOD

1. How does the Flood Myth relate to your life?

2. How do you withstand your rising troubled emotions?

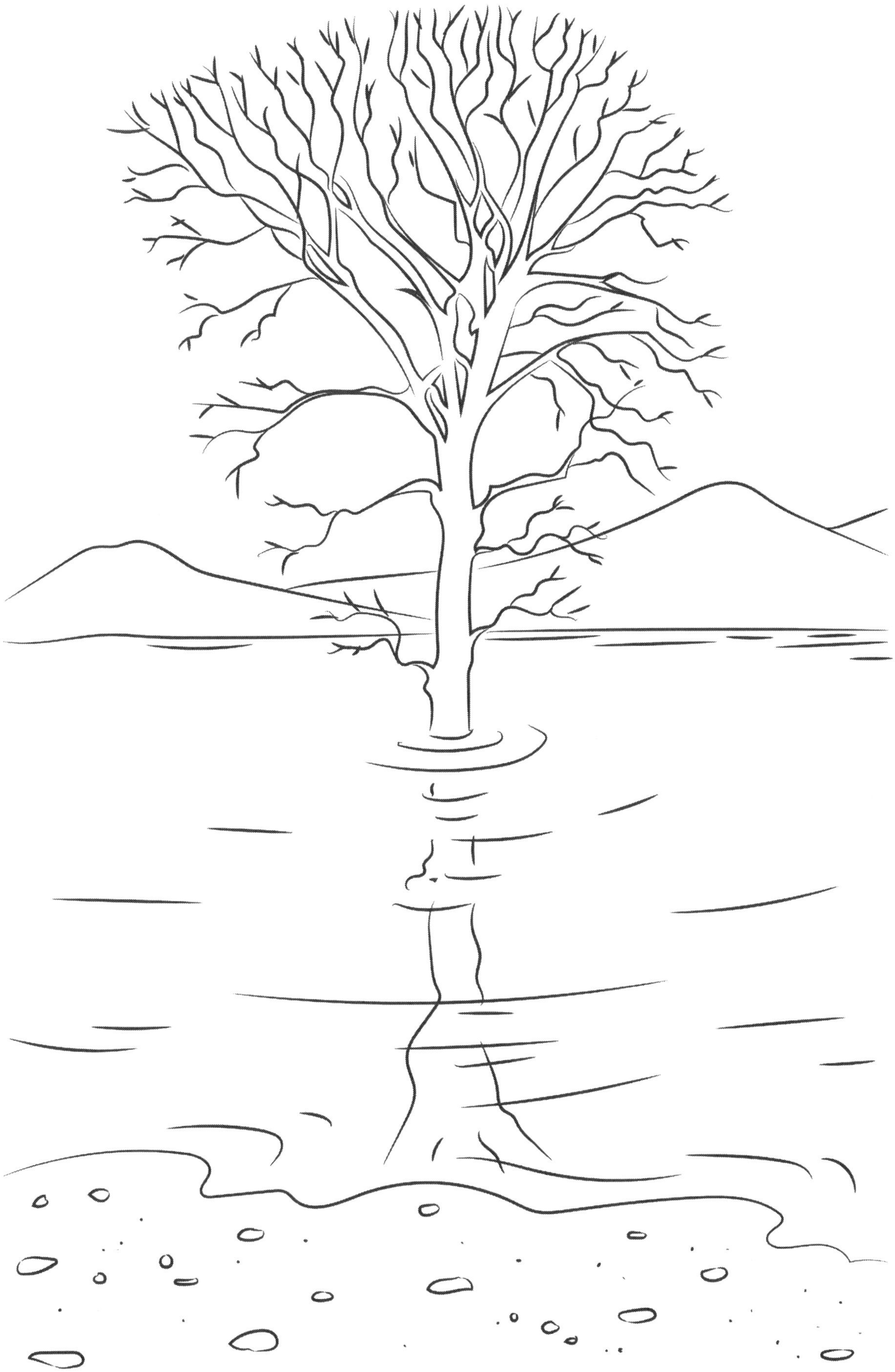

The Flower Myth

Flowers are a sign of impending spring. They enjoy rich traditions in mythic and spiritual writings and inspire reflection. *1 Peter 1:24-25* states, "all flesh is like grass and all its glory like the flower of grass. The grass withers, and the flower falls, but the word of the Lord endures forever."

Flowers often represent the archetypal (pattern or model) figure of the soul, which they share with butterflies. Carl Jung, in *The Structure and Dynamics of the Self*, writes, "the self can appear in all shapes from the highest to the lowest, inasmuch as these transcend the scope of the ego personality in the manner of a daimon [guiding spirit]. The principle plant symbols are the flower and the tree." In *The Archetypes and the Collective Unconscious*, Jung writes, "the symbol of the self is the circle elaborated into a flower (rose, lotus) or a wheel." Frequently this circle is found in the mandala, which is the last mythic image in this coloring book.

Gods and Goddesses are often related to flowers. H. G. Baynes writes in *Mythology of The Soul* that "the flower is the womb which gives birth to gods." In the Hindu tradition, Vishnu rests on the coils of the cosmic serpent of eternity, Ananta, in the waters of chaos, and he releases a lotus stalk from his navel which opens to reveal the creator god Brahma, who will create the world anew. The Egyptian Sun-god was also believed to have been born out of the lotus stalk and to have spent his childhood in the lotus flower. The symbol of the golden flower is an attainment of the highest spiritual state. Richard Wilhelm writes in *The Secret of the Golden Flower* that "when all is quiet and the spirit has continuously and uninterruptedly enjoyed great joy as those intoxicated, the light-principle is harmonious in the whole body [when] the golden flower begins to bud." The lotus' special admiration comes from its nature. Arising unsullied from mud and murky waters, it blossoms into a radiant beauty in the sunlight. It closes at night and opens in the morning, reborn resplendent in all its glory.

In *Qur'ān 50:7* is written, "and the earth is spread out and set thereon mountains standing firm and producing every kind of beautiful growth." Great goddesses rule over food plants that spring from the earth. Erich Neumann writes in *The Great Mother: An Analysis of the Archetype* that she is "frequently associated with a vegetable symbol: in India and Egypt with the lotus; as Isis, Demeter, or later the Madonna with the rose." In the *Mythology of All Races: Chi-*

nese Mythology is written, "the pomegranate and the lotus, on account of the large number of seeds which their fruits contain, are symbolic of offspring." Reflecting nature and its cycles, mother Demeter and daughter Persephone are goddesses of corn and grain. Persephone dies each winter (kidnapped and taken to the underworld) only to be released to revive spring (*The Golden Bough: A Study of Magic and Religion*). She is reborn through the magical powers of pomegranate seeds.

Flowers signify many meanings depending upon their color. As examples, white is purity and innocence but also funereal offerings; red is vitality and blood; blue is fervent devotion (Lord Vishnu is a blue god); yellow is the sun; and golden flowers represent perfection, etc. The mythology of the flower is as prolific in number as they are lush in beauty. The human divine is opened in their fullness and souls fly to the thrones of gods.

QUESTIONS FOR REFLECTION AS YOU COLOR THE FLOWER

1. How does the Flower Myth relate to your life?

2. In what soil does your soul flourish to become its golden beauty?

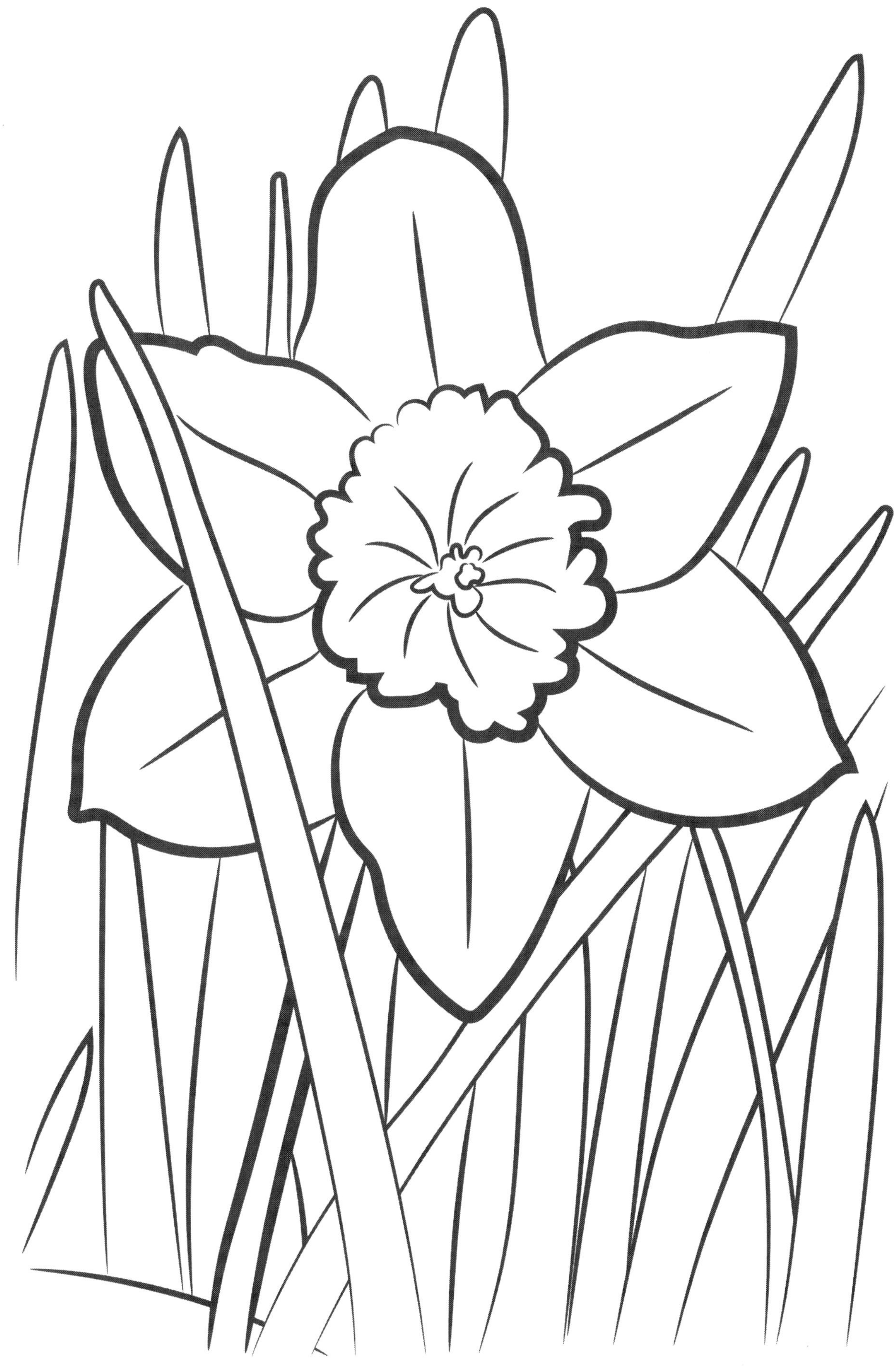

The Garden Myth

Gardens are a symbol of tranquility, reflection, awe and spirit.

In the intimacy of hands entering the earth, sifting and turning it, seeds and botanical cuttings are planted to be nurtured by the soil. The vision of their profusion gives solace to every gardener. In mythology, paradise is a garden and it symbolizes a perfection of cosmic order. Flowers are the sure sign of spring.

Gardens are a verdant refuge from the outside world and give respite from day-to-day problems, strife and concerns. We abandon ourselves to laughter in them. Their visual design gives order to an unordered world. They delight one's eyes whether they are part of the smallest backyard space or expansive private or public lands. They are a physical space that reflects an inner wholeness with their conscious combinations of plants, trees, herbs and water. Flowing waters within enclosed Muslim gardens are an image of paradise. In the *Qur'ān 3:136*, the Prophet says, "For such the reward is forgiveness from their Lord, and gardens with rivers flowing underneath–an eternal dwelling: how excellent a recompense for those who work (and strive)!"

Psychologically, gardens reflect consciousness versus un-consciousness, an ordered nature versus the unordered wild growths of forests and hills. In gardens, humans find, as *Jeremiah 31:12* states that, "...their life shall become like a watered garden, and they shall never languish again." The garden is also a symbol of the soul as well as that of a mystical journey, which reflects an inner balance indicative of a state of spiritual harmony. Gardens, like the labyrinth, welcome the individual to find their center.

In mythology, gardens are found in mythical locations such as Elysium, Hesperides, the Isles of the Blessed or Blest [where the goddess Hera enjoyed a golden apple orchard, but, who ultimately had to place the serpent-dragon Ladon there to protect them from theft], as well as Avalon: *Insula Avallonis*–Isle of fruit trees. The apple tree is also found in Norse mythology where it confers immortality and perpetual youth. However, there is some speculation that the golden apple might actually have been an orange.

In Renaissance paintings, gardens often contain the Fountain of Youth where old people bathe in its waters, emerge young again and are reinvigorated. These artworks also include themes of blossoming love and sensory delights where the garden offers a secret refuge for romance.

In many designs, a garden can only be entered through narrow passageways.

These restrictions symbolize a barrier from the outside world where the individual may attain their highest spiritual manifestation inside.

The Garden Myth celebrates life's renewal. Even in the barrenness of winter, life will not be denied. Only humans lose hope and commit suicide. *Never so* with nature. A great quote from the movie, *Jurassic Park*, says it all, "life...finds a way." And it always will. It fights for every scrap of light and nutrient soil. If a lowly plant can blossom despite harsh conditions, how much more can we as divine human creations manifest?

QUESTIONS FOR REFLECTION AS YOU COLOR THE GARDEN

1. How does the Garden Myth relate to your life?

2. What keeps you from blossoming into the lushness of life?

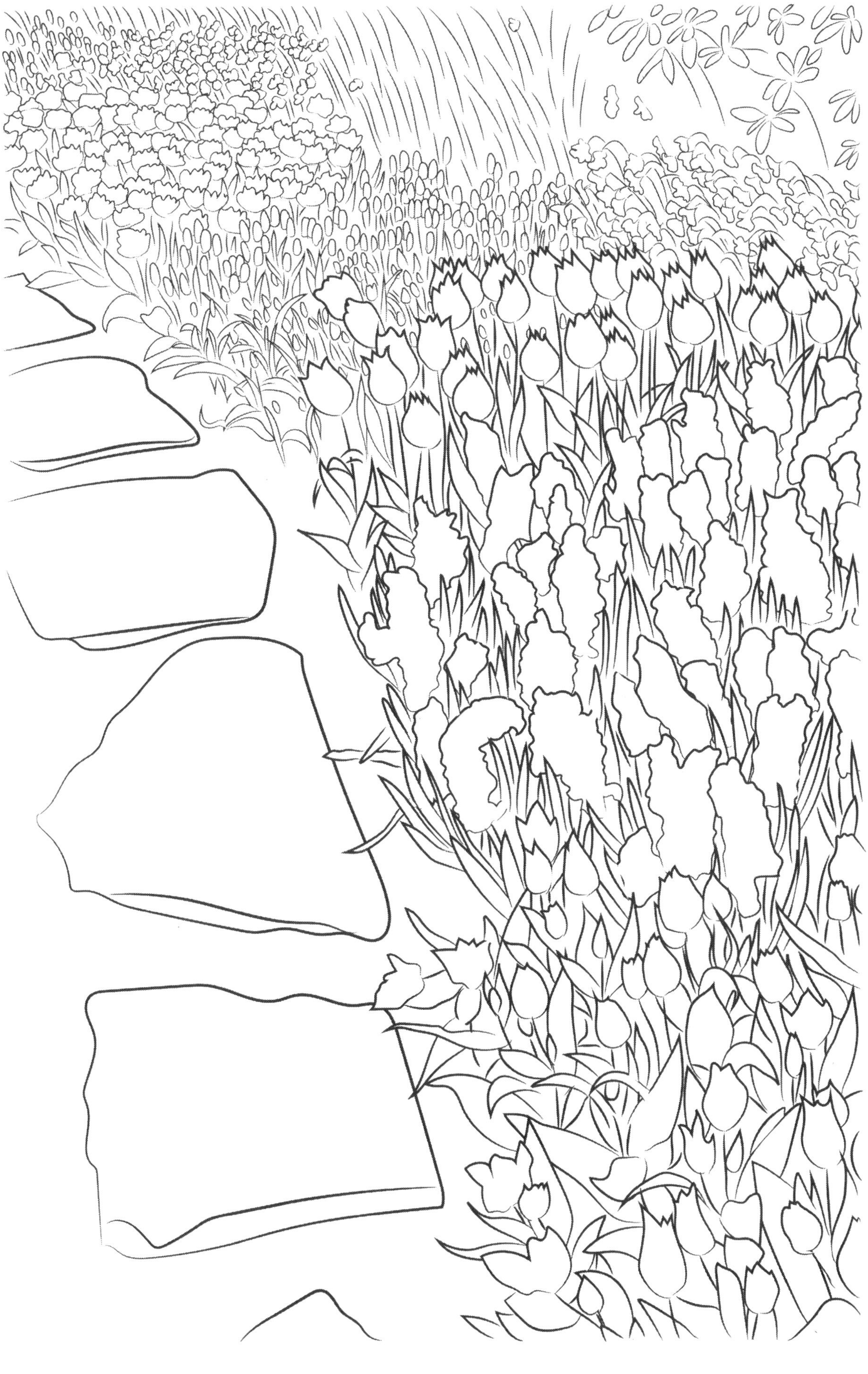

The Honeybee Myth

The Honeybee myth is one of being in sweet service to others.

Honeybees are universally seen as being industrious, diligent, clean and technically organized with special skills. The pollen that bees collect helps them produce honey; they also exude beeswax which they form into the hexagonal structure of the honeycomb. Both honey and beeswax are vital to the colony.

The honeybee has remained unchanged for 20 million years, with elder bees teaching the young. A single honeybee will visit 50-100 flowers during a single collection flight. Collectively 2 million flowers must be visited to produce a pound of honey. A healthy hive will house a population of about 50,000 honeybees. It is estimated that 80% of fruits, vegetables and seed crops are pollinated by honeybees.

Honey has been collected by humans long before the advent of agriculture over 9000 years ago. Mesolithic art depicts humans smoking bees out of hives in trees, bushes and caves to collect their honey. Ancient Egyptians were the first peoples to raise honeybees. They prized them for honey used as food for the gods.

Many classical goddess figures in ancient mythology are associated with the honeybee: Cybele (Central Asia Minor), Artemis and Demeter (Greece), Potnia (Minoan-Mycenaean), Nambi (Uganda), Austeja (Lithuanian), Colel Cab (Mayan), Melissa (Greek/Minoan) and Mellona (Roman). In ancient Egypt, honeybees represented the tears of the sun-god RA. In Islamic, Middle-Eastern, Aryan and Greek myths the honeybee represents the soul. Also, Hindu gods Vishnu and Krishna are called "nectar-born" gods.

The honeybee is also a figure of death and rebirth.

During winter months they disappear only to fly out of their hives in spring to stimulate new life. Folklore describes them as "birds of paradise" because they can produce wax for sacred candles, make honey for humankind and their hive's humming song worships God. The Celts, among others, imagined the honeybee to have wisdom and share the immortality of the soul. The beehive also symbolically represented the early Catholic Church.

In *The Group and the Primal Horde*, Sigmund Freud considered the analogy of the honeybee's ability of turning a single bee larva into a queen instead of a worker as being that of "transforming group psychology into an individual psychology." Carl Jung observes in *The Structure and Dynamics of the Psyche* that when the honeybee arrives back to the hive it does its "direction dance," teaching the other bees the direction and distance of pollinating flowers. He notes that, "this kind of message is no different in principal to single humans teaching others what they have learned."

The honeybee's life is similar to the Hero's Journey as eloquently outlined by the renowned mythologist Joseph Campbell in *The Hero with a Thousand Faces*. Each honeybee leaves the hive (home), goes forth in search of flowers (adventure and challenges), collects pollen (life experiences), and returns to the hive (society) to create honey (sharing wisdom). And like us, honeybees are vigilant and ferocious against any attack to their hive as we are to our many homelands.

QUESTIONS FOR REFLECTION AS YOU COLOR THE HONEYBEE

1. How does the Honeybee Myth relate to your life?

2. How do you share the sweet wisdom of your life?

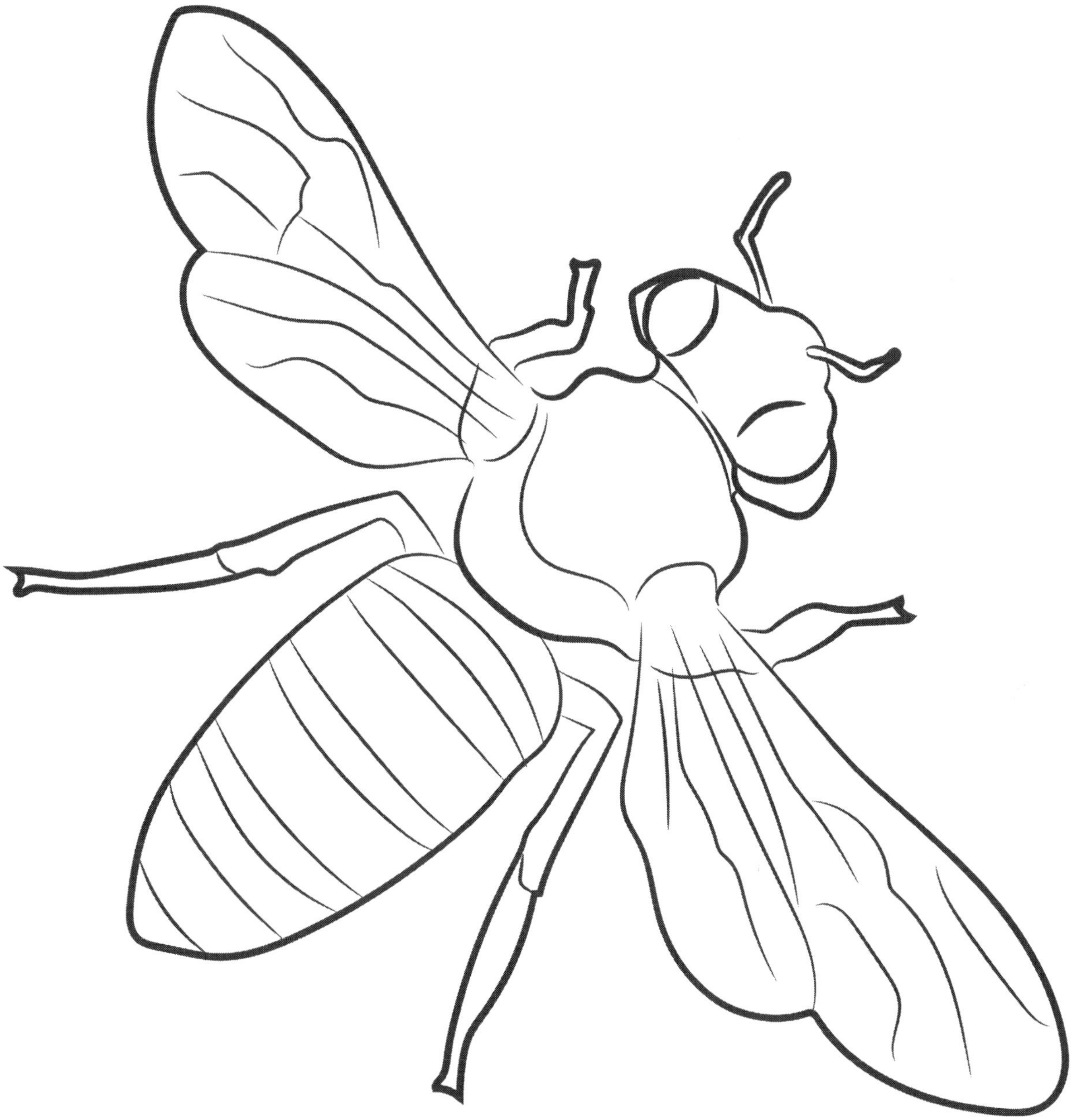

The Key Myth

A key is a tool that allows you to lock or unlock important objects, such as a door or treasure chest.

On a practical level, keys also lock or unlock gates, storehouses, safety deposit boxes, prison cells, psychiatric wards, and file cabinets storing important items, etc.

Psychologically and emotionally, keys allow us to know our deepest truths, defenses and impulses, such as suddenly realizing a key principle to the depth understanding of our own beliefs. We seek "key truths" in the writings and sayings of others which may impart wisdom that can empower our lives as it has theirs.

Keys are also used metaphorically to keep people in their own "mental prison constructs." We may feel that "bad" individuals who offended, insulted or hurt us deeply are to be punished, so we "lock them away." One problem with this is that we must continue to expend a great deal of energy to keep them there by being a "vigilant prison guard." This is a huge price for unforgiveness—understandable as it is. If we ever want to reclaim that squandered energy for our own healing, envision using a key that releases them…and us.

In the Eagles song, *Already Gone*, some of the lyrics express the Key Myth perfectly, "…so often it happens that we live our lives in chains, that we never even know we have the key." It may rub us wrong to free those who have hurt us but do they know or even care? We can never change the past, only process it. A life of bliss is when some people are not in it any more, except as an invaluable lesson of those not healthy for us.

Within mythology, keys have been viewed as instruments that open sacred worlds in religious and written works, such as the "keys of the kingdom." These symbolic keys allow the initiated to enter heaven and paradise; or, keys can be withheld to refuse admission to those not initiated or who are unbelievers. *Matthew 16:19* says, "I will give you [Saint Peter] the keys of the kingdom of heaven, and whatever you bind on earth will be bound in heaven, and whatever you loose on earth will be loosed in heaven." In *Qur'ān 6:59*, "With Him are the keys of the Unseen, the treasures that none knoweth but He. He knoweth whatever there is on the earth and in the sea. Not a leaf doth fall but with His knowledge: there is not a grain in the darkness or the earth, nor anything fresh or dry but is in a record clear to those who can read." In *Homer's Odyssey, XXI:6-10* we read that Persephone, "In her stout hand took hold of the well-curved key, a lovely one of bronze. And an ivory handle was on it. And she went on with her serving women into a chamber, the last room, where the treasures of her lord were lying, bronze and gold and iron that was highly wrought."

In *Symbols of Transformation,* Carl Jung writes that, "...the key unlocks the mysterious forbidden door behind which some wonderful thing awaits discovery." In *The Symbolic Life,* Jung writes, "the ancient mystery cults are always connected with psychopompic deities. Some of the deities are equipped with the keys to the underworld (as with Hecate), because as the guardian of the door they watch over the descent of the initiates into the darkness and are the leaders of the mysteries."

QUESTIONS FOR REFLECTION AS YOU COLOR THE KEY

1. How does the Key Myth relate to your life?

2. What are the names of people kept in your prison, starting with yours?

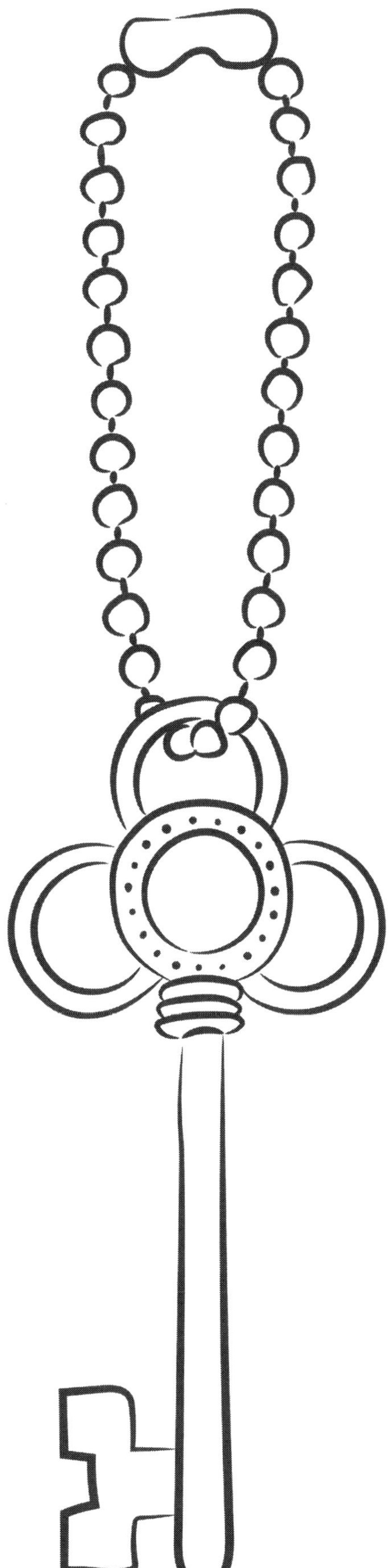

The Labyrinth Myth

The labyrinth is an ancient symbol of finding one's psychological center.

Labyrinths date back to the Paleolithic age and are found in cave paintings. A labyrinth is a very complex design that has a rich heritage in religious and meditative ceremonies, inspiring insights from both. The labyrinth design has also been used architecturally in medieval defensive designs around and within courtyards of ancient homes and cities. Some of the earliest known uses of labyrinths, in Egypt and Etruia (central Italy), provided protection for the tombs of kings. Pagan folk dances, which dance to the center and then out, are the spiral labyrinth dance of death and rebirth.

Labyrinths are primarily two main designs, the unicursal and the multicursal design (cursal: belonging to a set course or direction). The most typical design today is the unicursal, or *one* circular (spiral) design. Celebrating the labyrinth generally begins by a person becoming conscious of their breath before stepping into the space and focusing on their intention (i.e., conscious problem solving, anxiety reduction, spiritual connection or pleasure). The person enters the path, walks in a contemplative manner surrendering to the experience. Pausing at the center for any insights, wisdom or guidance gained, the person retraces the circular path back to where they entered.

The labyrinth design is mirrored in seashells, whirlpools, eddies of streams and rivers, spider webs, coiled serpents and especially in the intestines of mammals. Entrails of sacrificed animals were often used for divination purposes. In ancient Rome, a person trained to "read" livers of sheep and chickens was called a haruspex. The "exit of the bowels" was understood to be the place of birth, where the Bible describes birth as a separation from the bowels. *In 2 Samuel 7:21*, "and when thy days be fulfilled, and thou shalt sleep with thy fathers, I will set up thy seed after thee, which shall proceed out of thy bowels, and I will establish his kingdom." Sigmund Freud writes in *Revision of Dream Theory* that, "I cannot resist pointing out how often light is thrown by the interpretation of dreams on mythological themes in particular. Thus, for instance, the legend of the labyrinth can be recognized as a representation of anal birth: the twisting paths are the bowels and Ariadne's thread is the umbilical cord."

Freud's mention of Ariadne is a reference to one of the most widely known mythological labyrinth stories. In the myth, King Minos, son of Zeus and Europa, was the first king of Crete. His daughter, Ariadne, was put in charge of the palace's underground labyrinth. As restitution for the killing of Minos' son, Athens had to send seven young men and women each for seven years to Crete. Once there the men and women were to be killed and eaten by the Minotaur (a monstrous man with the head of a bull). One year the sacrificial party included a handsome young man, Theseus, the son of the Athenian King Aegeus. Theseus had volunteered to kill the Minotaur. Adriane fell in love with Theseus and provided him with string and a sword, with which he killed the Minotaur. The string, used to lay down a return path through all the convoluted twists and turns of the labyrinth, enabled Theseus to follow the string back to the upper world of light.

Finding a way out of a problem by going into it is central to many sacred and psychological texts. This is the function of the labyrinth.

QUESTIONS FOR REFLECTION AS YOU COLOR THE LABYRINTH

1. How does the Labyrinth Myth relate to your life?

2. What wisdom path leads you to the essence of your Being?

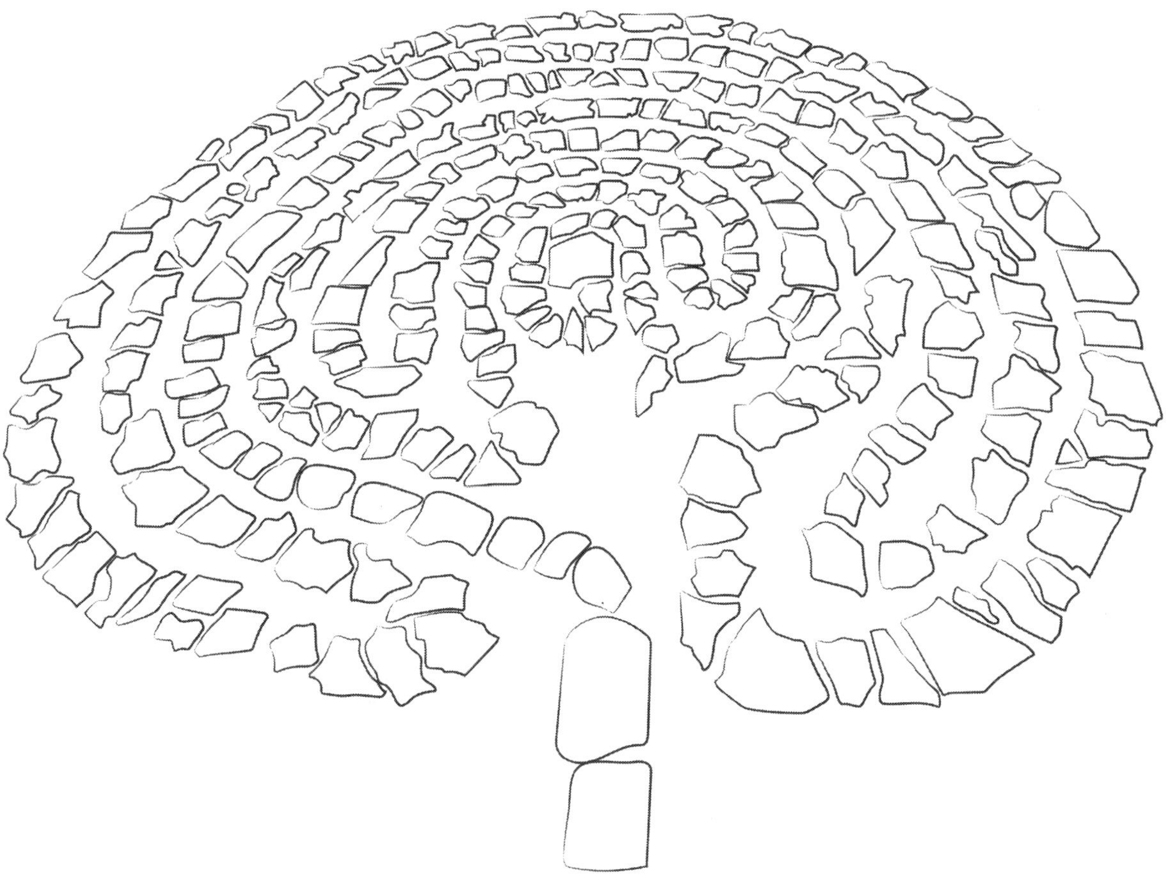

The Moon Myth

The Moon is a symbol of reflection and it exerts a profound influence in the mythologies of every culture.

It is a lover's inspiration, a song's reflection and a shadow's ghost. From ancient lore, the moon has been the basis of the first calendars that described the passing of time as being measured by successive and regular cycles. Most death-rebirth gods in mythology and religion take their inspiration from the three nights of total darkness, with the god's descent into the underworld or death, and their rising reborn on the third day (new moon). These phases of the moon give us the symbolic inspiration for dualisms. The moon, especially in the ancient Orient, has a greater significance than the sun which never changes. Ancient hunters used the moon as a nocturnal source of light besides hunting in the light of day.

The moon is usually represented as being a female deity, except in Japanese, Oceanic, Sumerian and Teutonic cultures. In Greece, the tri-form goddess of the New, Full and Old Moon relates to the virgin, woman and crone phases of the moon. Dr. Margaret Merisante writes, "Moon goddesses appear all over the world. Some examples include Greece—Artemis and Selene; Italy—Diana and Luna; China—Chang-O; Yoruba, Africa—Yemoja; Aztec and Central America—Coyolxāuhqui; Hawaii and Pacific Islands—Hina; and Mama Killi—Inca and South America among others." Look for her upcoming book on goddesses.

The sun and moon together represent the sacred marriage (*hieros gamos*) of heaven and earth. The eclipse of the sun is related by Joseph Campbell in *The Hero with a Thousand Faces* as a Hindu myth of the cup of immortal life-nectar being pursued by the beheaded titan, Rahu. His head manages to swallow the cup but it passes easily through his mouth and out again through his throat, during which time the cup (moon) disappears.

The moon is closely associated with female fertility, rain and moistness. Besides menstruation, it influences all bodily fluids in females and males. The moon influences the tides and growing cycles in nature depending upon its waxing or waning moon cycles. Native American Indians had a planting moon.

Emergency room staff will confirm that irrational, eccentric behavior peaks at the time of a full moon. The Roman moon goddess Luna is the origin of the word lunacy and lunatic. Carl Jung writes in the *Symbols of Transformation* that, "most forms of lunacy consist of affections which amount to an invasion by the unconscious and an inundation of the conscious mind."

Besides symbolizing immortality and eternity, the moon also represents the dark side of nature. Because it rotates identically to the Earth, only the light "near side" is seen, the "dark side" is always hidden. This gives rise to psychological interpretations of our unconscious mind and insightful humor. Mark Twain writes, "Everyone is a moon and has a dark side which he never shows to anyone." In the movie, *Star Wars*, Darth Vader tries to entice Luke Skywalker when he says, "Give yourself to the Dark Side. It is the only way you can save your friends."

QUESTIONS FOR REFLECTION AS YOU COLOR THE MOON

1. How does the Moon Myth relate to your life?

2. Do your soul waters reflect the luminosity of your life wisdom?

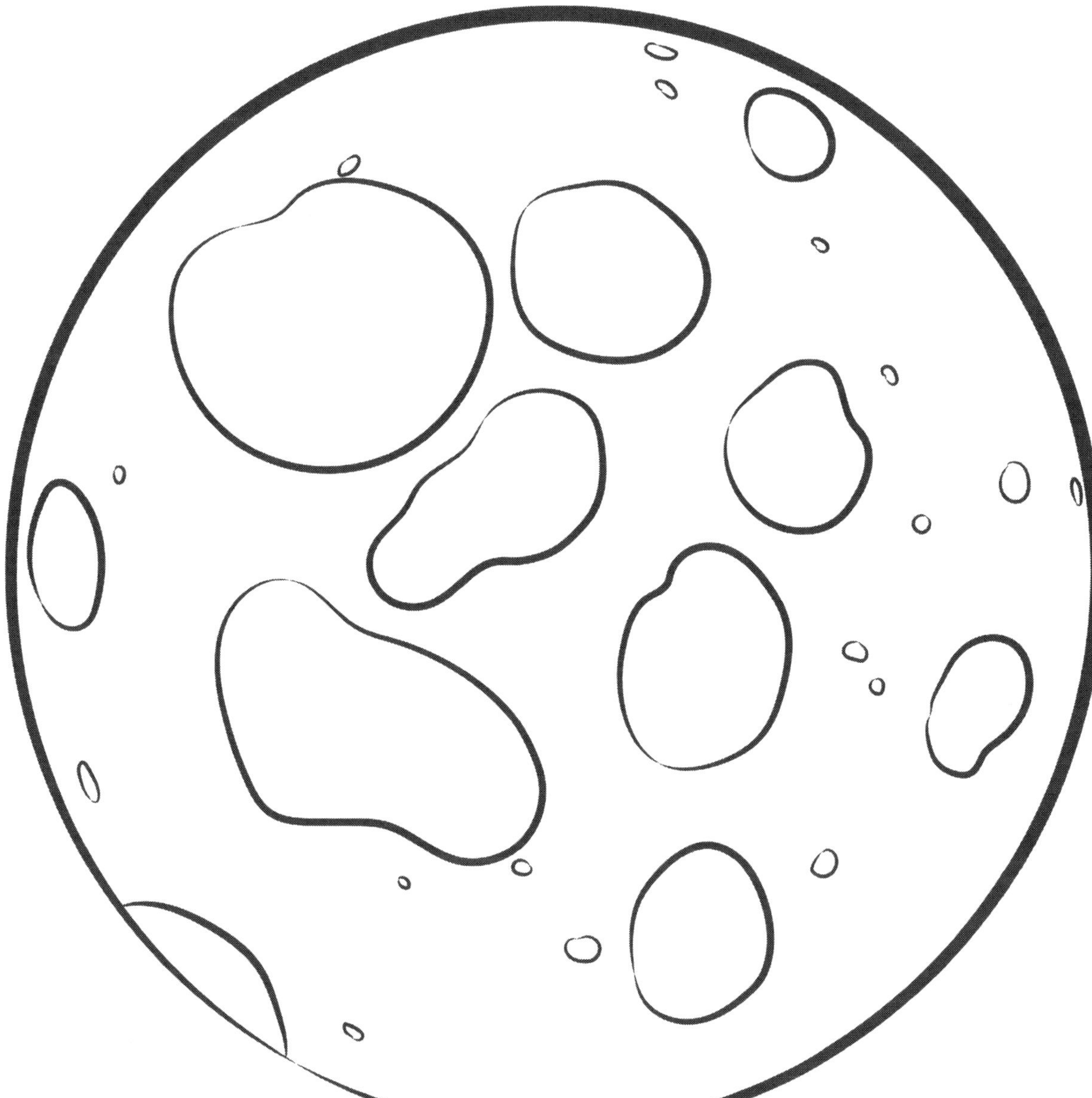

The Mountain Myth

Mountains are symbols of immovable stature and influence.

Being eternal, stable and impermeable, mountains represent transcendence, manifestation and connections between earth and sky. They are the dwelling places of giants, dwarfs, fairies, gods and immortals. In them are heroes waiting to be called—such as King Arthur, Merlin and Barbarossa. The darker side of mountains includes death and destruction with volcanic eruptions such as Mt. Vesuvius and Mount St. Helens.

For those undertaking the arduous effort of climbing mountains, the climber may strive to achieve a sacred character, a connection with the numinous (spiritual, if not magical) and a journey to the realm of spirit with a peak experience at the summit. The climber becomes one with the mountain's mass and verticality. Mircea Eliade writes in *The Sacred and The Profane* that, mountain "images express the connection between heaven and earth; hence it is believed to be at the center of the earth." Pilgrimages up sacred mountains require a renunciation of comfort, worldly concerns and often personal safety.

Religious temples, Mesopotamian ziggurats, Egyptian pyramids, Buddhist stupas, Asian pagodas and Hindu vimanas are in many ways human re-creations of the "Cosmic Mountain" with its *axis mundi* (world axis/center of the world/navel of the earth). Holy mountains inspired tablets of law to ancient Babylonian kings and to Minoan Crete rulers, a concept later adapted into the legend of Moses on Mt. Sinai.

The mountain is one of the oldest images of gods, generally male but with exceptions of the mother goddesses in Asia Minor, India and Crete (Cybele and the Minoan great goddess Parvati). Her mountain snowmelt and rainfall gave rise to rivers and streams fertilizing everything downslope. In *Memories, Dreams, Reflections*, Carl Jung wrote of his experience in the American Southwest with Navajo Pueblo peoples. One wisdom elder asked Jung, "Do you not think that all life comes from the mountain?" Jung looked at the nearby mountain with its river surging downwards and he agreed, saying "Where there is water, there is life."

Some of the best known sacred mountains are: Kun-Lun and Li-ku-ye in China, Meru in India, Fuji-yama in Japan, Olympus in Greece, Alborj in Persia, Sarizam of the Samaritans, White Mount of the Celtic British Isles, Moriah in Genesis, Potala in Tibet and Montsalvat in the Grail Legend. In *The Divine*

Comedy, the poet Dante Alighieri places the earthly paradise (Garden of Eden) on the summit of Mount Purgatorio (Purgatory).

Mountains have been referred to in many sacred texts. In *Psalm 30:7* "By your favor, O Lord, you have established me as a strong mountain." In *Psalm 36:6* "Your righteousness is like the mighty mountains..." Religious worship was often celebrated on high places. Examples include the upper level of Babylonian ziggurats, within small caves around the Acropolis rock and atop the Klepsythra spring as far back as the Neolithic period of 3,000 BC.

QUESTIONS FOR REFLECTION AS YOU COLOR THE MOUNTAIN

1. How does the Mountain Myth relate to your life?

2. What exuberance dances on the majesty of your mountain?

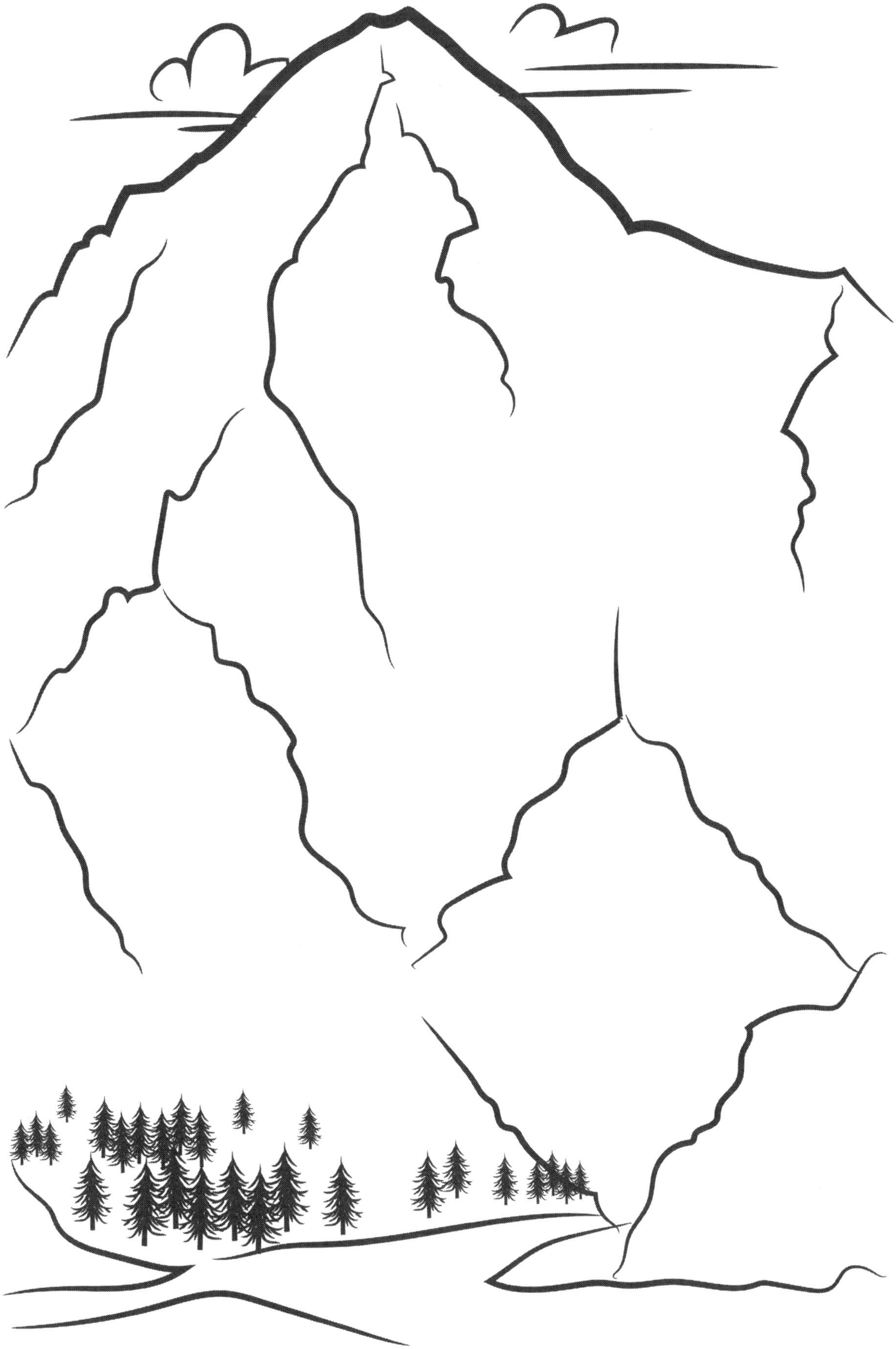

The Stairs Myth

Stairs, stairways and ladders are symbols of the ascent to the divine.

They share common themes of enlightenment, initiation and transcendence. They represent the upward pathway to spirit and absolute reality. Descending ladders or stairs may symbolize occult knowledge, mystery and magic. Joseph Campbell writes in *Occidental Mythology: The Masks of God* that the stairway or tower of the ziggurat "was not meant to storm and threaten heaven, but to provide a means by which the gods of heaven might descend to receive the worship of their slaves on earth."

In the beliefs of our forebearers, steps are symbols of ancestral rites. With these the priest, king or ruler transcended profane (irreligious) space and entered sacred space. Ascending stairs, levels or steps (as with long staircases on ancient temples) was to exert oneself in order to attain heaven and to acquire divine knowledge, i.e., as above, so below. At each level, the initiate became transfigured by a growing sense of enlightenment. This also held for descents in temples to levels below the surface of the ground for hidden truths.

The Sumerians were the first to construct ziggurats (brick mountains). These were followed by Akkadians, Babylonians and Assyrians; each ziggurat structure having 2 to 7 levels. The ziggurat at Babylon was called *Etemenanki* (Foundation of Heaven and Earth). The earliest Egyptian step-pyramids were close in design to a ziggurat. A thousand years later, the Mayan and Aztecs also built stepped pyramids. In a footnote, Egyptian scholar E. A. Wallis Budge notes in *The Book of the Dead* that, "The allusion [reference] is to Osiris who sat upon the top of the stairs at Abydos." Abydos is one of the oldest cities of ancient Egypt and the site of numerous temples.

The origin of the word "stairs" draws upon the Old English words *staeger* (stair) and *stigan* (to climb). In *Memories, Dreams, Reflections,* Carl Jung writes how he had entered a house in a dream that he did not know, but that it was "his house." The first level was of a modern home with hundred-year-old furnishings. He took a stone stairway down to a cellar with its vaulted room of Roman times with chips of brick in the mortar. Continuing, he then walked down narrow stone steps to a level cut into bedrock. Here he found in the thick dust scattered bones, two half-disintegrated human skulls and broken pottery. All were the remains of a primitive culture. He reflected that the house represented "the concept of the collective unconscious."

Mircea Eliade concluded in *Patterns in Comparative Religion* that the idea of an "ascension" into heaven by means of either a rope, tree or ladder was widespread in all five continents. And in *The Rites of Passage*, Arnold Van Gennep also notes that for the Irtysh Ostyak (Siberians) the other world is in the sky and is reached by ascending ladders. For the ancient Egyptians, Osiris was the "God of the Stairs." Finally, in *Genesis 28:10*, Jacob dreamt "...that there was a ladder set up on the earth, the top of it reaching to heaven; and the angels of God were ascending and descending on it."

QUESTIONS FOR REFLECTION AS YOU COLOR THE STAIRS

1. How does the Stairs Myth relate to your life?

2. How do you ascend to the wisdom of your divine Higher Self?

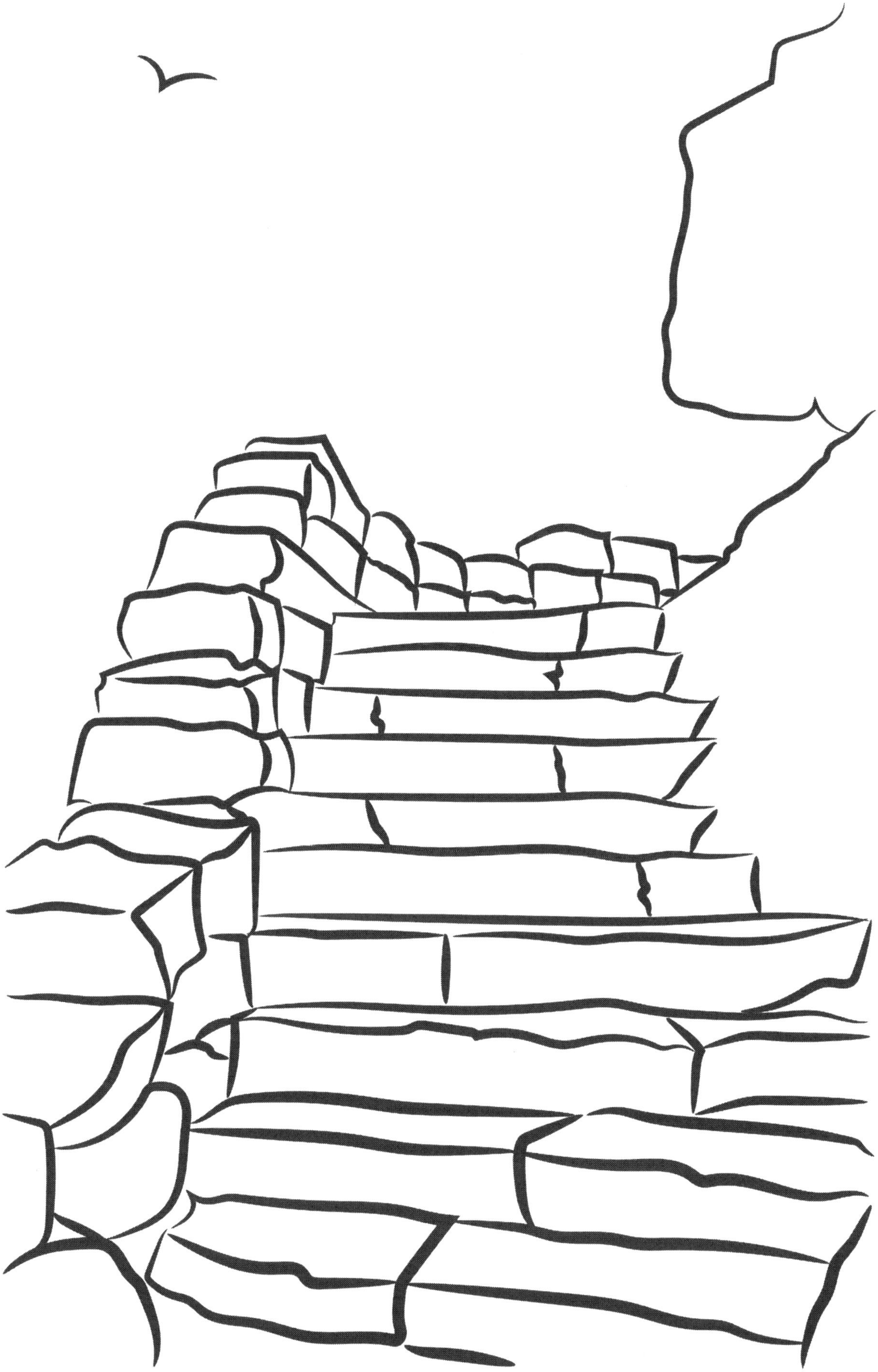

The Stone Myth

The mythology of stone is universally defined by its hardness, strength, endurance, motionlessness and ruggedness.

In our daily language, whatever is written "in stone" is unchangeable, while to be unfeeling is to have a "heart of stone." As symbols of permanence, stones are commonly used as grave markers of the deceased. Being permanent and resistant, stones are believed to provide protection from hostile powers and forces. Mircea Eliade writes in *Patterns in Comparative Religion* that, "all places where saints lived, prayed, or were buried are, in turn, sanctified, and are therefore cut off from the profane space around them by an enclosure or an embankment of stones." Tall upright stones were often regarded as a sacred *axis mundi* (the center of the world or world axis). One example is standing stones marking the spot where the umbilical cord of Zeus had fallen.

Stones have been used as both tools and weapons since the "Stone Ages." Because they store heat, from prehistoric times, ancient peoples put hot stones into animal bladders filled with water to boil meat and other food items, making them tender and digestible.

Stones are used worldwide for worship. Altars are made of stone, especially marble. Meteorites have been especially regarded as messages from gods, as well as being a dwelling place of the deities. Standing stones with mineral veins in them are venerated greatly and are perceived as being alive. We still "worship" these standing stones when we visit Stonehenge or various menhirs in Europe and elsewhere.

In an ancient Greek myth, before Zeus was to send a great flood to punish humankind for its wickedness, Prometheus warned his son Deucalion and his wife (and cousin) Pyrrha to build an ark. They survived and after nine days found dry land. Deucalion and Pyrrha were advised by the goddess of prophecy, Themis, to cast stones over their shoulders as they walked the land. Those stones cast by Deucalion became males, and those cast by Pyrrha became females. In this way, humanity was renewed.

In many early religious traditions, temples were only constructed using unhewn stone. In *Exodus 20:25*, we read, "But if you make for me an altar of stone, do not build it of hewn stone; for if you use a chisel upon it you profane it." In *Deuteronomy 27:6*, we read, "You must build the altar of the Lord your God of unhewn stones."

Erich Neumann writes in *The Origins and History of Consciousness* that,

"...diamond, stone, or rock, as symbols of self, represent the indestructibility and permanence of something that can no longer be split apart by the opposites." The opposites here can be seen as a psychological analogy of the alchemist working with the "philosopher's stone" (turning base matter into gold) but with the "base matter being our personality," to achieve an integration of the masculine conscious self with the feminine unconscious self, thereby transmuting psychic elements into an essence of wholeness and individuation.

QUESTIONS FOR REFLECTION AS YOU COLOR THE STONE

1. How does the Stone Myth relate to your life?

2. What hardness and endurance is to be chiseled out of your archaic lineage?

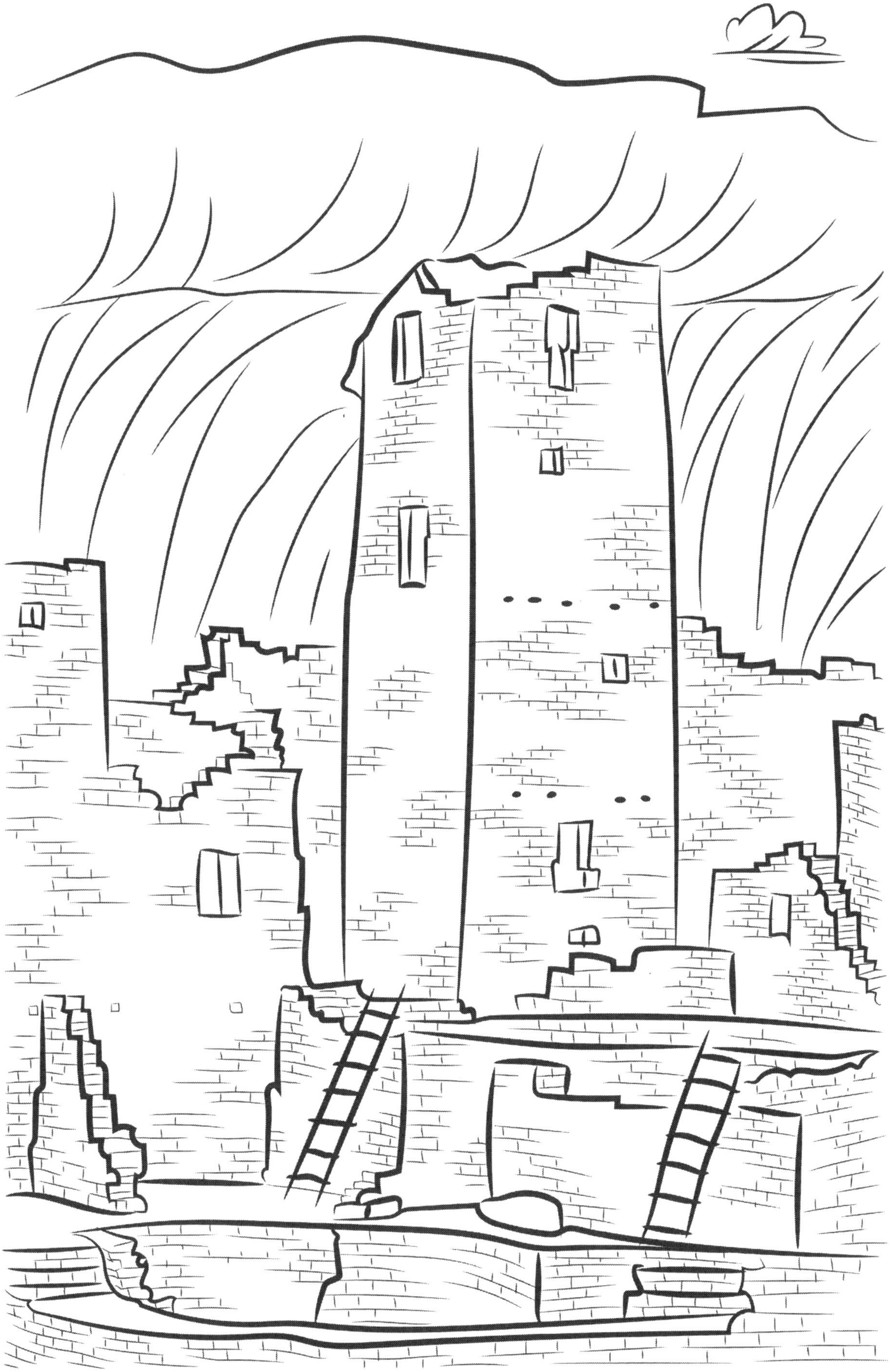

The Threshold Myth

Thresholds symbolically represent a transition, or transcendence, from one stage or passage of your life into another.

Threshold symbolism has a rich tradition in entertainment, religious beliefs, marriage ceremonies and psychological meanings. In movies, a threshold guardian is the character who tells the hero that she or he is not ready for their hero's journey. If the hero listens, they will live their life forever unfulfilled and die full of regret. But when they embrace their innermost spirit and proceed regardless, they overcome all obstacles and challenges to obtain the happy ending. A hero realizes that to live a fully manifested life, they must go forward despite all consequences. In this way, they live life adventurously. They become their own mythic hero.

In religious beliefs, the threshold represents a passage from the profane (irreligious) to the sacred or to a source of a blessing. Thresholds in Christian cathedrals are laden with many figures whose function is to separate the profane world "outside" to the sacred one "inside." In *Ezekiel 47:1*, the prophet saw "water flowing from below the threshold of the temple toward the east..."

In the East, doorway thresholds are carved with "keepers of the threshold" in the form of dragons and effigies of gods or spirits. In Mali, the Bambara summon their ancestors by striking the threshold with a stick, which is carved to represent them. The single-tusked elephant god Genesha is a threshold guardian and gatekeeper. He is the Hindu god who removes obstacles and is a benefactor to writers and students. Sisiutl, the two-headed serpent monster, is a Pacific Northwest American Indian figure. When he is painted on entry doors with his menacing glare, he protects the homes by turning any intruder into stone.

Ancient marriage ceremonies regarding thresholds had symbolic meaning for young couples. The groom protected his bride from bad spirits living under the doorstep when he carried her over the threshold. In Zoroastrian and Brazilian faiths, the groom must step with his right foot over the threshold without touching it. In Bulgaria, the bridal couple both ensure that they enter the church by stepping inside with the right foot first over the entrance. "Putting your best foot forward" seems to be a logical origin of this saying, though nothing definitive exists substantiating it.

Another couple's stillborn child was often buried under a threshold to ensure that the second couple's first child would be alive and healthy. James Frazer, in *The*

Golden Bough, writes that in Northern India, when a child dies, it is usually buried under the threshold of the house "in the belief that as the parents tread daily over its grave, its soul will be reborn in the family."

Carl Jung writes in *The Structure and Dynamics of the Psyche* that, the "unconscious contains all those psychic events which do not possess sufficient intensity of functioning to cross the threshold dividing the conscious from the unconscious." Sigmund Freud, citing Herbert Silberer, writes in *The Interpretation of Dreams* that the state just before awakening, may be understood in terms of "crossing a threshold, leaving one room and entering another, departure, a home-coming..."

QUESTIONS FOR REFLECTION AS YOU COLOR THE THRESHOLD

1. How does the Threshold Myth relate to you?

2. Despite intimidating gates and threshold guardians, how will you summon the courage to move into the next phase of your life?

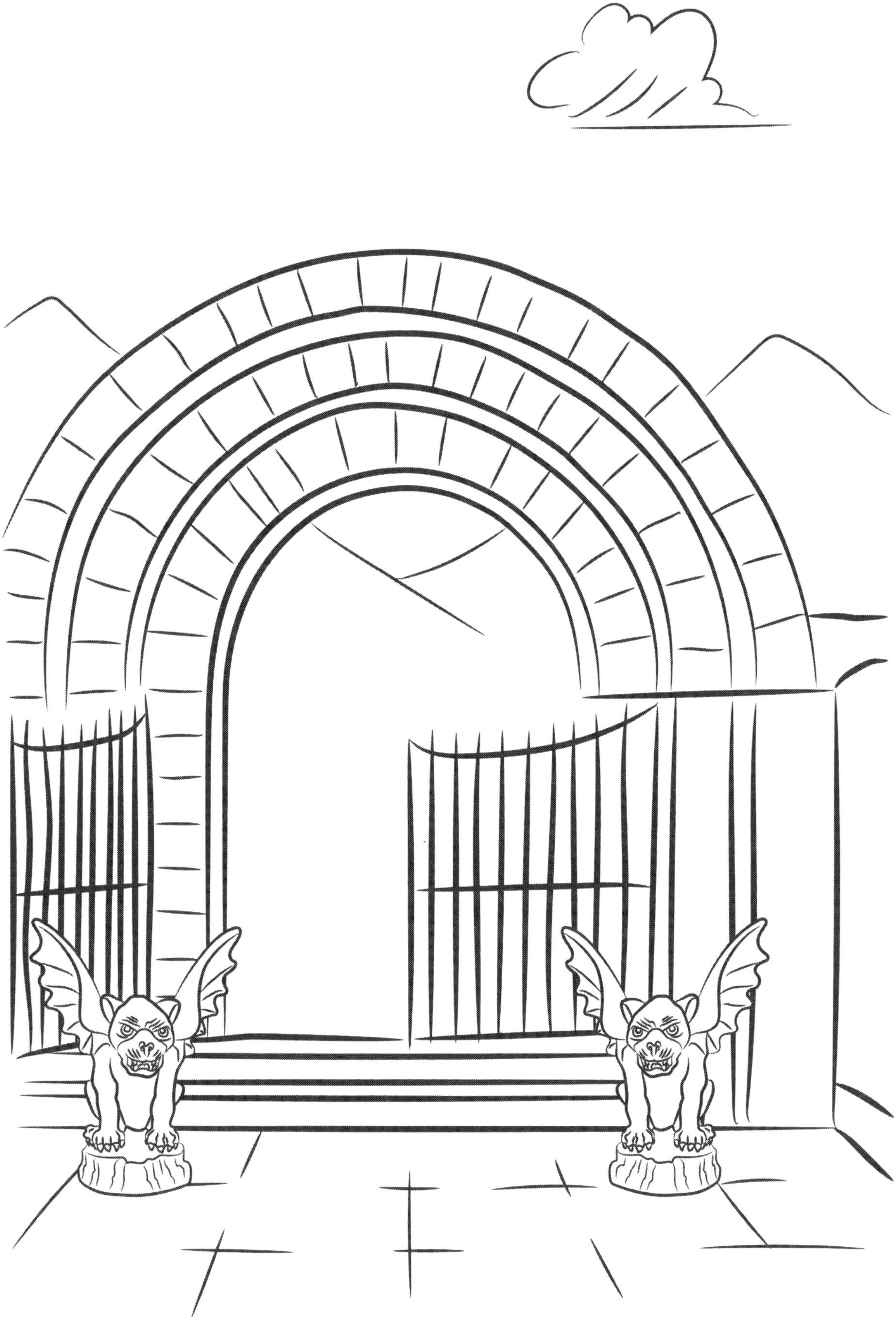

The Tree Myth

The Tree myth dates back to pre-Neolithic times and is a universal worship symbol.

It is no wonder that we are psychically connected to trees. When we were a fetus in the final months in the womb, we could see the branching of veins and capillaries outlined against our mother's translucent skin. As children and adults, looking up through the canopy of a tree, we again see the same pattern of branching. The deep regard for trees being both familiar and maternal is a function of this prenatal experience. Look at the Tree Myth to color. Compare the mother's veins with the tree's branches; see how they mirror each other!

Carl Jung writes in *Symbols of Transformation* that, "...the tree is predominantly a mother-symbol." Trees often represent mother goddesses because of their life sustaining bounty. Examples include: the goddess Hathor of Egypt and the Sumerian goddess Inanna or Ishtar with the sycamore (fig), the Greek goddess Artemis and the palm tree, the Aegean triple goddess (who evolved into the Olympian Hera) and the pomegranate tree, and the Anatolian goddess Agdistis and the almond tree. These are but a few female deities who represented the fertility, abundance and nutrition of nut and fruit trees.

Trees represent life, both in its physical and spiritual sense. Additionally, because of their upward growth they are the model for human manifestation. With roots delving deeply into the soil, the tree binds itself with the earth and by its strong trunk and spreading crown, it integrates the underworld, earth and heaven. Carl Jung writes in *Alchemical Studies* that, "taken on average, the commonest associations to its meaning are growth, life, unfolding of form in a physical and spiritual sense, development, growth from below upwards, and from above downwards, the maternal aspect (protection, shade, shelter, nourishing fruits, source of life, solidity, permanence and firm-rootedness), but also being "rooted to the spot," old age, personality and finally death and rebirth." Deciduous trees lose their leaves in the winter and sprout them again in the spring thus representing resurrection.

R.E.L. Masters and Jean Houston write in *The Varieties of Psychedelic Experience* that LSD/peyote users they studied had "a major revelation that was of the spiritual nature of trees: the obedient benevolence of trees. One was obliged to commune with them and with statues. This imperative was part of a larger imperative that seemed to stand out absolutely from all other thought as the one overriding imperative statement: That one must seek God."

The Tree of Life and the Tree of Knowledge are all central points of the divine cosmos: the *axis mundi* (center of the world/world tree). They confer immortality and wisdom by their nature.

Fire is believed to be hidden within trees, which can be extracted by rubbing one piece of wood against another. This is the way that early humans created fire: rubbing a wood stick against a wood base until friction ignited it. Dry softwoods such as pines work best. If a fingernail can dent the wood, it is soft enough to make fire. Two softwood pieces work best, but a piece of hardwood can be used for the stick.

QUESTIONS FOR REFLECTION AS YOU COLOR THE TREE

1. How does the Tree Myth relate to your life?

2. Meditate on the Fetus and Tree images.
Is there an ancient memory of being in the womb?

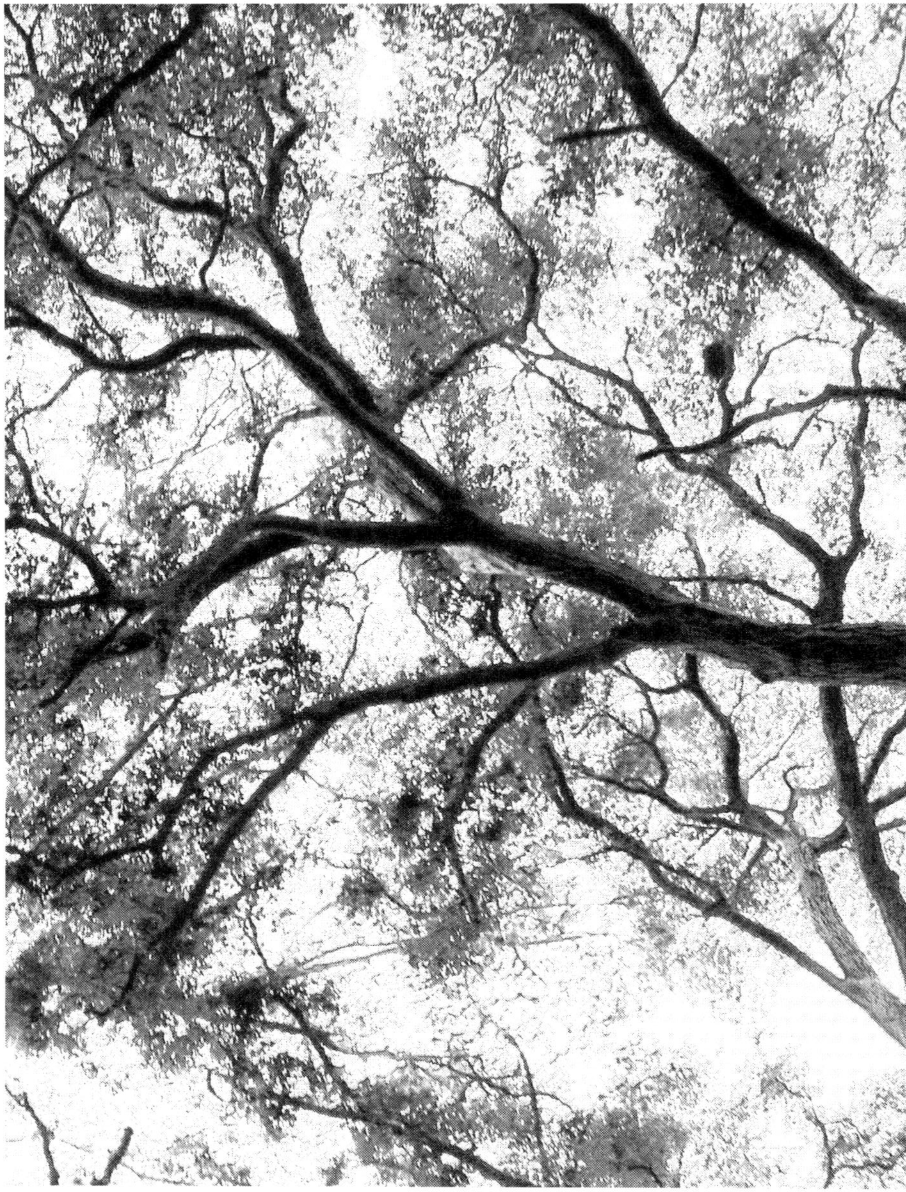
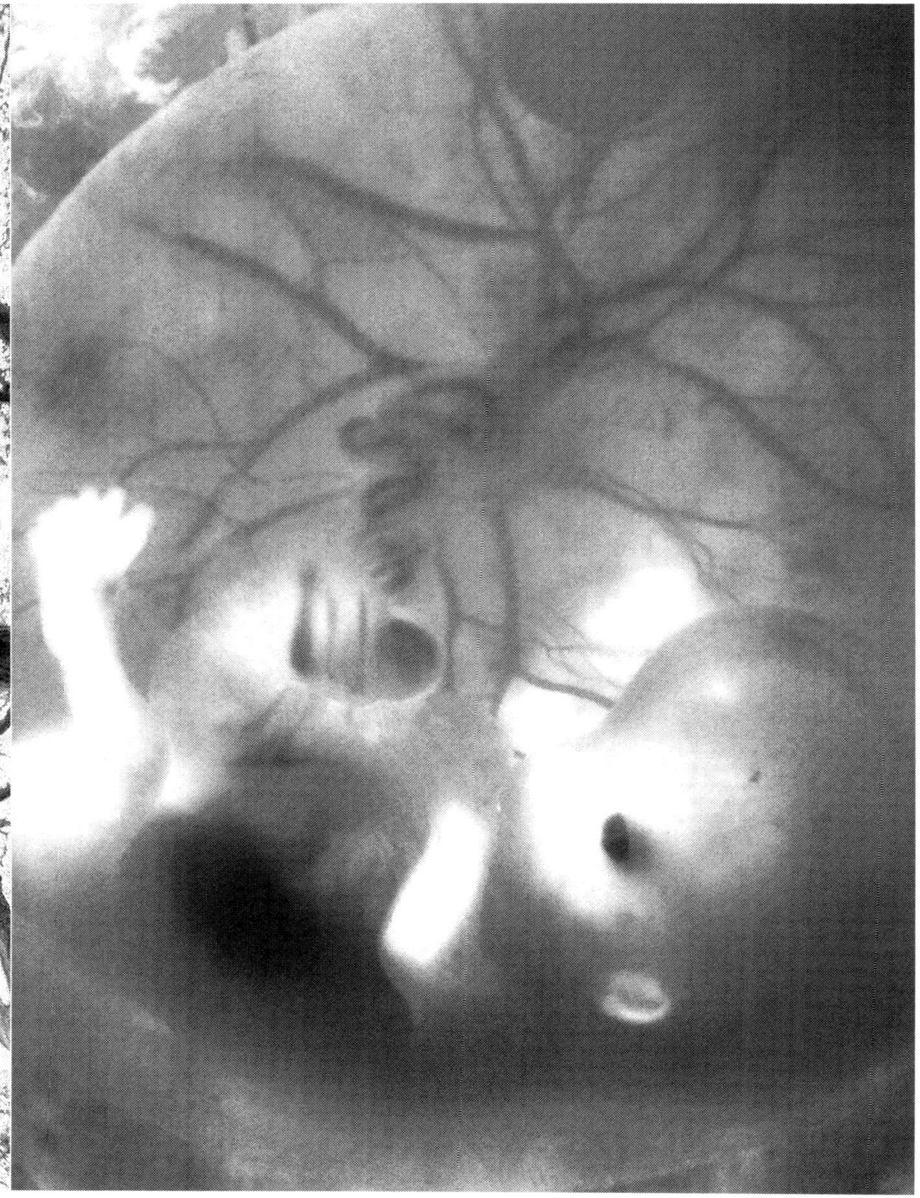

Actual Photos

The Water Myth

The Water myth is a symbol of fertility and life.

Three-fourths of our bodies are comprised of water. A fetus in the womb floats in a salty amniotic fluid. Water is unparalleled as a source of fertility and purity for all living matter. In humans, it is an emblem of all fluidity: amniotic fluid, blood, tears, sweat, saliva, semen and menses.

Water, by its nature, is formless representing the infinite nature of all things. It symbolizes not only life, but death. Rain is essential for all lifeforms and yet, in its raging aspect, heavy rains sweep away all life and create mass destruction. Water's sweet nature is found in its freshness and its bitter nature is found in salty oceans and seas—and from pervasive pollution from human negligence and utter disregard for consequences beyond the moment.

Mythological figures abound around water. In China, water is the abode of the dragon whose rain provides all life. The Egyptian deity Nu was the first of nine gods that emerged from the primordial abyss of water, and from two of them a male and female human were fully formed. The watery abyss in Mesopotamia was regarded as a symbol of unending wisdom. The Egyptian god of rebirth, Osiris, was revived by the tears from Isis and Nephthys which flowed over him. Tammuz-Adonis, an Asiatic god of plants and springs, brings new vegetative life from the ground. In ancient Babylon, the primordial goddess of salt sea, Tiamat, mated with Apsu, the god of fresh water, to produce Lahmu and Lahamu. In Hindu texts, Agni is born of waters, Varuna controlled waters and Vishnu not only slept on the waters but grew a lotus enthroning Brahma from his navel. Not surprising for a desert people, in the Biblical and Islamic traditions, water signifies mercy.

In *The Hero with a Thousand Faces*, Joseph Campbell tells a myth from the North American Pueblo Indians. Water Jug Boy was a source of unusual gifts. He was born from a young woman as a little jug. In time, he grew big and was able to walk and talk with other children as they matured. In its fullest manifestation, and in its essence, the jug holds life for others so that they may thrive.

Water is used to dissolve impurities in and from matter. This concept has a spiritual nuance in absolving, purifying and "washing away" sins and other transgressions. The ancient pagan rite of baptism is extensively used today in many modern religious and initiatory ceremonies that consecrate new life, decree membership or redeem those "fallen from grace." Other religious contexts include "crossing the stream" to in order to attain enlightenment or Nirvana. And, the boundary river Styx is crossed at death in order to enter the Greek underworld. When Caesar brought his legions back to Rome to ultimately become dictator, he had to cross the River Rubicon. The saying "to cross the Rubicon" now means to "pass a point of no return."

The transparency of water allows it to be considered a medium of obtaining wisdom and divination. Nostradamus wrote his quatrains from visions in a dark vessel of water. Water's natural mirror-like quality allows it to be a window into the soul for those seeking hidden knowledge.

QUESTIONS FOR REFLECTION AS YOU COLOR THE WATER

1. How does the Water Myth relate to your life?

2. A single droplet and the vast ocean share the same nature. How has your uniqueness been formed by the collision with the immensity of humanity?

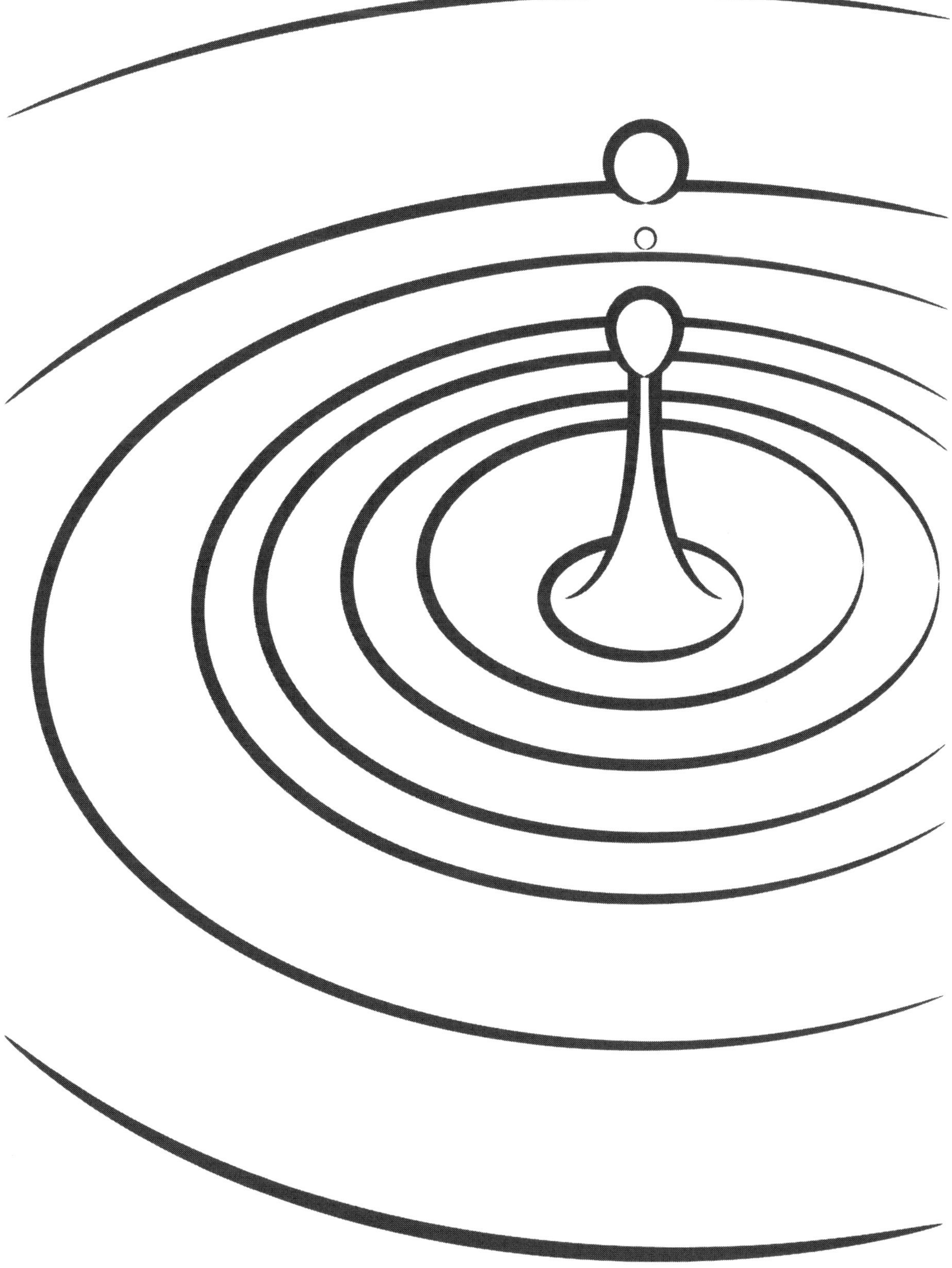

The Mandala Myth

The Mandala is a simple design of a circle within a square, yet it represents the profound expression of your spirit and being.

I will discuss how to complete this mandala image at the end of this section. As Edward F. Edinger writes in *The Eternal Drama: The Inner Meaning of Greek Mythology*, "the whole body of mythology serves this mirroring function."

The word "mandala" is Sanskrit for *circle*, and more especially, "a magic circle," according to Richard Wilhelm, translator of *The Secret of the Golden Flower*. The first known mandalas from about the 9th to 10th century were discovered in China. According to Susanne F. Fincher, author of *The Mandala Workbook: A Creative Guide for Self-Exploration, Balance, and Well-Being*, the Sanskrit word "mandala" also means "a complete cycle through time." She suggests that the zodiac is one of the most widely known versions of this temporal cycle.

Mandalas often symbolically elicit a religious or therapeutic experience. They are intended to be used in meditation by you, its creator; they can serve as instructional tools, protective talismans or ritual objects. Besides that, they are beautiful and reflectively insightful no matter the artistic skill. Robert A. Johnson writes in his *Inner Work: Using Dreams & Active Imagination For Personal Growth* that, "the self has characteristic symbols: the circle, the mandala, the square, and the diamond are all abstract figures that express the archetypal self." Mircea Eliade writes in *Images and Symbols* that, "placing the neophyte in a mandala, like a Navajo Sandpainting, may be likened to the initiation by entry into a labyrinth." The Navajo sandpainting mandalas used by the shaman-medicine man invoke and exalt the *Yeibicheii*, or Holy People, to heal the sick person sitting in the middle of the sacred mandala sandpainting.

In *The Symbolic Life*, Carl Jung writes that a mandala arises from "the deepest impulses of our essence," and, "in the center of the magic circle or sacred precinct is the temple [you]." In *Memories, Dreams, Reflection*, Jung writes, "When I began drawing the mandalas, however, I saw that everything, all the paths I had been following, all the steps I had taken, were leading back to a single point—namely, to the mid-point. It became increasingly plain to me that the mandala is the center. It is the exponent of all paths. It is the path to the center, to individuation." Marie-Louise von Franz contributes a chapter in Carl Jung's *Man and His Symbols* where she writes, "The contemplation of a mandala is meant to bring an inner peace, a feeling that life has again found its meaning and order." In *Ego and Archetype*, Edward F. Edinger writes, "the mandala is the major symbolic expression of being an individual." Jolande Jacobi adds in *Complex/Archetype/Symbol*, that the mandala communicates "the sensing of a center of personality, a kind of central point within the psyche..." And as Jean Houston encourages in *A Passion For The Possible*, "if you are feeling low and without purpose, go mythic!"

Joseph Campbell writes in *The Flight of the Wild Gander* that, "it is the province of art...[that it is] a quest for, and formulation of, experience-evoking, energy-waking images yielding...a sensuous apprehension of being." Reflecting this thought, Candace B. Pert writes in *Molecules of Emotion* that, "...getting to deeper more fundamental levels of accessing our emotion includes storytelling, hypnotherapy, neurolinguistics programming, and any of the expressive therapies that employ visualization, music and art." Otto Rank writes in *Art and Artist* that, "...creativity begins with the individual—that is, with the self-making of the personality into the artist." In *Analyzing Children's Art*, Rhoda Kellogg describes how drawing mandalas comes naturally to us as children. "Initially a two-year old with pencil or crayon just scribbles, but soon seems to be attracted by the intersection of lines and begins to make crosses. Then the cross is enclosed by a circle and we have the basic pattern of the mandala."

Stanislav Grof writes in *The Adventure of Self-Discovery* that, "we like to combine Holotropic Breathwork with a mandala drawing as was developed by Joan Kellogg, a psychologist and art therapist. The procedure is very simple: the subject is given a set of crayons or magic markers and a large piece of paper with the outlines of a circle, and is asked to fill the circle in any way that seem appropriate. It can be just a combination of colors, an abstract composition of geometrical patterns, or a more-or-less complex figurative drawing." Cut-out pictures from magazines and publications are also used and pasted within the circle to render the breather's experience visually.

Now is the time for your mythic adventure by working on your own mandala.

In the center of the circle is "YOU." Write your name through it. Write inside the circle words or phrases arising from your insights from any of the mythic images you have colored. Beside words or drawings, you might also want to glue pictures or symbols from periodicals and magazines that fit inside the circle, or outside "the sacred circle of you" if you do not want them to be a part of your life. The blank mandala in this coloring book is limited in size. However, the same mandala design can be re-drawn on much larger paper that will allow many more images to be glued that represent your insights. Sheets of paper from easel pads used in meetings, or by presenters, are ideal for this purpose.

Your mandala expresses your deepest truth through art. Embrace the child inside you who has a sense of play.

After you have finished your mandala, perhaps you might want to place it in front of you as you do an "open-eyed" meditation. Look at it as you breathe: reflect on your life, where you have been, where you are now and where you want to be.

The adventure into your own life essence is yours to engage. Have fun with it! Your personal mandala will astound you. I hope that you do many creative mandalas in the future.

QUESTIONS FOR REFLECTION AS YOU COLOR THE MANDALA

1. How does the Mandala Myth relate to your life?

2. What ecstasy thrives in your Soul center?

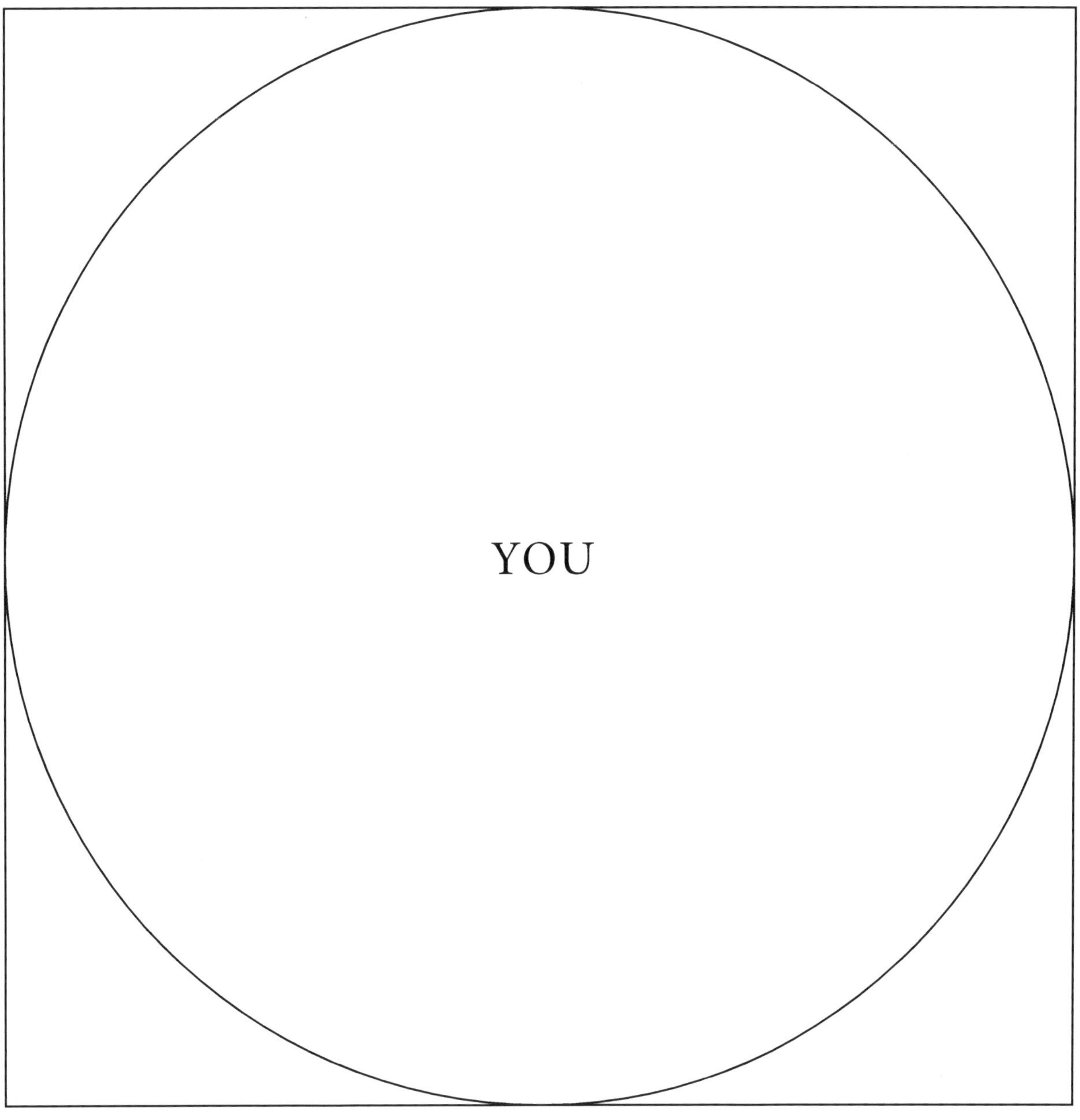
YOU

Last Reflections

It is my hope that you may have been deeply moved by coloring the various mythic images, and especially, the Mandala myth. "Last Reflections" presents valuable insights from recommended authors for reflection on personal mythic stories that you've discovered.

In *The Surrender Experiment*, Michael A. Singer suggests that, by "surrendering to the unfolding of life you let go of any self-limiting demands that the world around you manifest itself according to your likes and dislikes." People create their own misery this way. Participate in life's flow. You are one with the psyche of our species. In honoring its life wisdom, you honor yours. You are, and have been, all you need to be. "Each of us may be but a small drop in the flow of life but together we form the ocean of common humanity." In sharing your life legacy, you gift the universe, family and friends your path to self-realization that can be a model of service for others.

Meditation is the access to this heritage.

In *The Art and Science of Mindfulness*, Shauna L. Shapiro and Linda E. Carlson offer a path to deep inner knowing. "Outcomes are linked with intention: that each meditation be of service to you. May I be safe. May I be happy. May I be healthy. May I live with ease." Empathy is a wonderful by-product of mindful meditation and the one person who most needs it is likely to be you. We are connected to each other and all life forms when we honor ourselves and others. We heal ourselves with these connections. As a side benefit, "it has been found that meditators offset the detrimental effects of normal aging on cortical thickness [the outer layer of our brain]."

Meditation is a book of consciousness with chapters of your imagination.

"When you seek solutions to life problems, dance, drum, imagine, invoke, invite, draw or sing yourself a solution." This advice, and more, is to be found in Jean Houston's *A Passion for the Possible*. She refers to a gnostic quote in the Gospel of Thomas, found in *The Nag Hammadi Library*, "That which you have will save you, if you bring it forth from yourselves. That which you do not have within you will kill you if you do not have it within you." What is it that people do not have within? It is the *courage* to make that which is inside, in their dreams and vision, a new reality. To know that you have an unfulfilled purpose in life, or to know that there is something more to do in life than what you have already done, but do not to make that effort, is to endure a life of misery. Fear will seduce you into death-bed regrets. People who have richly fulfilled lives do the work to develop their talents. "By evoking new connections in brain, body, mind and spirit, sacred psychology brings one's entire self to a higher order," Jean Houston adds in another of her recommended books, *The Search for the Beloved.* "Your higher order is that which you came to earth to be and to serve."

Your dreams are your own soul talking to you. From an article in *Inner Knowing*, "Dreaming Consciousness," by Montague Ullman, MD, he writes that "dreams show ourselves with greater honesty and in greater depth than we normally allow." In his fascinating book *Hermes and His Children*, Rafael Lopez-Pedraza writes, "Dreams give us information, either clearly, obscurely, or in riddles, about our psychological state, the direction of our psyche, and even the prognosis of our life."

Your dreams tell you everything you need to know about yourself.

For those who say they can't record dreams, all you have to do is to drink a big glass of water just before going to sleep. You will have to relieve yourself in the middle of the night, but you will awaken from a dream to do so. Record your dream **first**, then relieve yourself. Otherwise, you'll forget most, if not all, of the dream by the time you come back to bed, especially the most elusively illogical and intriguing parts.

This is the method I have used for more than 40 years and I have recorded at least *one dream each night* during all those years. You, too, will soon compile a vast library of dream images, people, places and things...the images that make up the mythic story of "who you are."

Your soul is speaking to you in your dreams. Avoid dream dictionaries like the plague! They only tell you what *that* author thinks about some image or activity. It may be useful, but not likely. Develop your own dream dictionary, image by image, if that's important to you. Consider another's comments, but utterly reject what they say if they try to tell you "this is what your dream means." Trust that you "know what you know." If you do not wish to consult with someone professionally trained in dream work, then a book I highly recommend is Robert A. Johnson's *Inner Work: Using Dreams and Active Imagination for Personal Growth.* Another excellent book is *Conscious Dreaming* by Robert Moss.

Carl Jung writes in *Memories, Dreams, Reflections* that "Myth is the revelation of divine life in [humans]." Tell us your mythic stories by whichever expression works best for you, we're here to share your life's wisdom. Be the great love inside of you and...

Color yourself mythic!

91966493R00058

Made in the USA
San Bernardino, CA
31 October 2018